# How To Be A Christian Without Being Annoying

# How To Be A Christian Without Being Annoying

*Bette Dowdell*

*How To Be A Christian Without Being Annoying*

published by:
Confident Faith Institute LLC
PO Box 11744
Glendale AZ 85318
www.confidentfaith.com

First edition

© Copyright 2006 by Bette Dowdell
All rights reserved

No part of this publication may be reproduced, stored in a retrieval system or transmitted in any form or by any means (electronic, mechanical, photocopying, recording or otherwise) without prior, written permission.

Printed in Canada

ISBN: 0-9717728-0-0
LCCN: 2005905553

Cover Design: 1106 Design
Interior Design: The Printed Page

**Publisher's Cataloging-in-Publication**

*(Provided by Quality Books, Inc.)*

Dowdell, Bette.
   How to be a Christian without being annoying / Bette Dowdell. — 1st ed.
   p. cm.
   Includes index.
   ISBN 0-9717728-0-0

   1. Christian life.  2. Christian life—Biblical teaching.   I. Title.

BV4501.3.D684 2006       248.4
                                  QBI05-600092

# Dedication

*To Joanna and Matthew.*

*Raising you was the highlight of my life.*

# Acknowledgments

Well, where to begin? Daddy showed me what God might look like with skin on. All the people in all the Bible study classes I ever taught stretched me with their questions. Joe, Charles, Flo and Barney kept me appropriately humble, as required by the sibling handbook job description. Scott Combs made a lot of things possible. Many people encouraged me, including John Austerman, Suzanne Brand, Inajean Burcher, Jeff Duntemann, Barbara Fisher, Ted Gill, Jan Gitstein, Steve Harrison, Gwen Henson, Bob Kelly and Helen Perkins. Finally, the members of the Sunday School class I attend—Chris and Jen Forgey, Chris and April Lee, Sean and Cyndi McFarlin, Joe Pierotti, Mary Platt, and Rob and Carrie Worsham— make life better by laughing at my jokes.

My abject apologies to all those who richly deserve to be mentioned, but are not. Next time.

*Quotations used in this book come from the following versions of The Holy Bible:*

1. Contemporary English Version (CEV)
   *The International Student Bible for Catholics: New Testament Edition*
   Copyright © 1993 by Thomas Nelson, Inc.

2. *Good News Bible - The Bible in Today's English Version* (TEV)
   © Copyright 1966-1976 American Bible Society

3. King James Version (KJV)

4. *The Living Bible* (TLB)
   © Copyright 1971 owned by assignment by Illinois Regional Bank N.A. (as trustee) Used by permission of Tyndale House Publishers, Wheaton IL 60189 All rights reserved

5. "Scriptures quotes from *The Holy Bible, New Century Version* (NCV), copyright © 1987, 1988, 1991 by Word Publishing, Dallas Texas 75234. Used by permission."

6. "Scripture quotations marked (NIV) are taken from the *Holy Bible, New International Version*. Copyright ©1973, 1978, 1984 by International Bible Society. Used by permission of Zondervan Publishing House. All rights reserved.

   "The 'NIV' and 'New International Version' trademarks are registered in the United States Patent and Trademark Office by International Bible Society. Use of either trademark requires the permission of International Bible Society."

7. "Scripture quotations market (NLT) are taken from *The Holy bible, New Living Translation*, Copyright © 1996. Used by permission of Tyndale House Publishers, Inc., Wheaton Illinois 60189. All rights reserved"

8. "Scripture quotations marked (NRSV) are from the *New Revised Standard Version Bible*, © copyright 1989, by the Division of Christian Education of the National Council of Churches of Christ in the U.S.A. Used by permission. All rights reserved"

# Contents

| | | |
|---|---|---:|
| | Introduction | 1 |
| 1. | The Daddy You Always Deserved | 3 |
| 2. | A Child of God | 5 |
| 3. | What's So Original About Sin? | 7 |
| 4. | What Is This Thing Called Peace? | 9 |
| 5. | You Guilty Sinner You | 11 |
| 6. | Who Qualifies? | 13 |
| 7. | The Big Choice | 15 |
| 8. | A Brand New You | 17 |
| 9. | What Makes the Difference? | 19 |
| 10. | First You Walk | 23 |
| 11. | Celebrating What Is | 25 |
| 12. | Moving Past the Rule Pile | 27 |
| 13. | Obviously, Rules Are Not Enough | 29 |
| 14. | Hearing God's Voice | 31 |
| 15. | Ungames | 35 |
| 16. | Learning to Hear | 37 |
| 17. | Growing Up Is Good To Do | 39 |
| 18. | Working the Plan | 41 |
| 19. | Does Morality Count? | 43 |
| 20. | Walking Talks More Than Talking Walks | 45 |
| 21. | Where's the Power? | 47 |
| 22. | The Hold of Habits | 51 |
| 23. | How Far Do You Want To Go? | 53 |
| 24. | A Modern Day Tale | 55 |
| 25. | Strong Fingernails | 57 |

| 26. | Who Leads and Who Follows | 59 |
| --- | --- | --- |
| 27. | No Fence to Sit On | 61 |
| 28. | Why Bother? | 63 |
| 29. | Big Ideas, Weak Knees | 67 |
| 30. | Jesus – An Introduction | 69 |
| 31. | Trying To Put Jesus In a Box | 71 |
| 32. | Always a Two-Way Street | 73 |
| 33. | Who's In Control Here? | 75 |
| 34. | On Being Unique | 77 |
| 35. | Looking In the Wrong Direction | 70 |
| 36. | Maximum Defeat | 83 |
| 37. | Grave Clothes | 85 |
| 38. | Dead, Absolutely Dead | 87 |
| 39. | One Sunday Morning | 89 |
| 40. | A Credible Witness | 91 |
| 41. | Why? | 93 |
| 42. | Castles In the Air | 95 |
| 43. | Comparative Confidence | 99 |
| 44. | A Good Foundation Is a Solid Foundation | 101 |
| 45. | Don't Believe Everything You Hear About God | 103 |
| 46. | Don't Travel Alone | 105 |
| 47. | God Is Not Running for Sheriff | 107 |
| 48. | Everybody Believes In Something | 109 |
| 49. | Throw Away the Scale | 111 |
| 50. | Who Is Your Audience? | 115 |
| 51. | Status and Power | 117 |
| 52. | About This Forgiving Thing | 119 |
| 53. | Designer Gods | 121 |
| 54. | Shifting Sands | 123 |
| 55. | You Can Count On Consequences | 125 |
| 56. | Moving On Up | 127 |
| 57. | Parlor Tricks | 131 |
| 58. | One Way | 133 |
| 59. | Ignorance Is Not Bliss | 135 |

| | | |
|---|---|---|
| 60. | Beyond Physics | 137 |
| 61. | Don't Give Up and Don't Settle | 139 |
| 62. | It's All About the Finish Line | 141 |
| 63. | Crashing Through Life | 143 |
| 64. | The Liar's Liar | 147 |
| 65. | Both A Giver and a Taker Be | 149 |
| 66. | Being Clear On What Is Essential | 151 |
| 67. | Knowing Who We Are and What To Do | 153 |
| 68. | The Bible – Section #1 | 155 |
| 69. | The Bible – Section #2 | 157 |
| 70. | Accurate But Impossible | 159 |
| 71. | Same Words, New Tune | 163 |
| 72. | Real Christians Get Directions | 165 |
| 73. | Finding a Home | 167 |
| 74. | Hate the Sin, Love the Sinner | 169 |
| 75. | How To Get the Job Done | 171 |
| | Index of Articles | 173 |
| | Index of Scripture References | 176 |

# Introduction

Defining "Christian" might seem like describing a snowflake. There appear to be as many definitions as there are Christians. You probably know Christians who have something wonderful going on in their lives, while others lack the peace they should have and compensate by bugging the tar out of you. What makes the difference? How can you tell what's real?

Well, those questions are exactly why I wrote this book.

Christians, being people, are different from one another, but they have a common foundation, which the Bible describes in detail. Not everybody, though, understands all that's in the Bible. Some make it up as they go. But when people attempt to be Christian by willpower alone, they find it doesn't work—no matter how hard they try.

*How To Be A Christian Without Being Annoying* explains God's sure foundation. It shows the way to latch onto something authentic and powerful. People might still be annoyed because we're too tall, too short, too rich, too poor, whatever, but they'll know we're real.

This book has seventy-five, one-page "articles." Each will give you something to ponder, as will the brief excerpt from the Bible that accompanies it. The excerpts are a Bible sampler and give you an idea of the sort of information you'll find there. They come from different versions of the Bible to help you decide which version fits your style, and they let you know I didn't make up the stuff in the articles.

Read the book in any order. Start at the beginning and read to the end or "dip in" here and there to read about particular topics. Either way, enjoy your trip through these pages.

Please send your comments and questions to me at bette@confidentfaith.com.

                                        Bette Dowdell,
                                        Phoenix, 2006

# The Daddy You Always Deserved

*A*nyone who believes and says that Jesus is the Son of God has God living in him, and he is living with God. We know how much God loves us because we have felt his love and because we believe him when he tells us that he loves us dearly. God is love, and anyone who lives in love is living with God and God is living in him. And as we live with Christ, our love grows more perfect and complete…We need have no fear of someone who loves us perfectly; his perfect love for us eliminates all dread of what he might do to us.

- John's first letter, chapter 4, verses 15 through 18 (I Jn. 4:15-18)
- The Living Bible (TLB)
- Written in his later years by John, Jesus' youngest disciple. This letter was written shortly before he was exiled to the island of Patmos, in the Aegean Sea just west of what is now Turkey, where he lived out the rest of his life.

# The Daddy You Always Deserved

God describes himself as our father. Unfortunately, this loving description may create an obstacle for anybody who had a hurtful earthly father.

For whatever reason, some fathers don't do the parenting job well, so their children grow up never knowing a father's love. As a consequence, they believe they have little or no value. If they had value, they reason, Daddy would have loved them.

They may experience what passes for a father's love as a control device to make them jump higher, try harder. And high is never high enough. Hard is never hard enough. Daddy means being not quite good enough.

Or it may be that nothing from their father remotely resembles love because he was abusive—physically, sexually, mentally, emotionally. Here, daddy means pain.

If you grew up with a daddy who loved you for sure, you have a tiny little idea of what God is like. If you grew up without such a daddy, you need to put away your idea of what daddy means and get it behind you.

God is the daddy you always deserved.

You were always worth loving. You're worth loving now. Tomorrow and tomorrow and tomorrow, you'll still be worth loving. Until the end of eternity.

That's not to say God loves everything you do. The way you live your life may break his heart.

But God loves you.

# A Child of God

*S*ee how very much our heavenly Father loves us, for he allows us to be called his children—think of it—and we really *are*! But since most people don't know God, naturally they don't understand that we are his children. Yes, dear friends, we are already God's children, right now, and we can't even imagine what it is going to be like later on. But we do know this, that when he comes we will be like him, as a result of seeing him as he really is.

- John's first letter to the church at large, chapter 3, verses 1 through 2 (I Jn. 3:1-2)
- The Living Bible (TLB)
- John and his brother, James, both disciples of Jesus, came from a well-to-do fishing family. At the start of their time together, Jesus called them "sons of thunder" because of their explosive tempers.

# A Child of God

Not everybody is a child of God.

Many assume being God's child is somehow an automatic part of our genetic code. If we are all created equal, we must all be God's children. Right?

According to the Bible, no. Being a child of God is not automatic—for a very positive reason. God gives us freedom to live life as we choose. We are not obligated to a relationship with him. We have the option of living life with or without God.

The downside of this freedom, of course, is making the lesser choice. Lesser because we can discover all that our life was intended to be only when we live as God's child.

The good news is, anybody can become God's child. There's no magic or hocus-pocus to it. No barriers. No "earning your stripes." No secret password. Just a simple decision that's what you want to be.

It's very easy. In fact, amazingly easy. The actual decision takes an instant. You can do it anywhere, any time, in any circumstances.

But it changes everything.

This decision is the first step in a journey that will last a lifetime. And then some.

It starts you on your daily walk with God. It makes God your father, and allows him to lead you on your path to godliness. Your path to life as God intended it to be.

# What's So Original About Sin?

*G*od makes people right with himself through their faith in Jesus Christ. This is true for all who believe in Christ, because all people are the same: All have sinned and are not good enough for God's glory, and all need to be made right with God by his grace, which is a free gift.

- Romans, chapter 3, verses 22 through 24 (Rom. 3:22-24)
- New Century Version (NCV)
- Paul's letter to the church at Rome. Written in preparation for his first trip to Rome, this letter is an organized presentation of Paul's theology. In his letters, Paul uses the circuitous Greek logic of the day, which takes some understanding now.

# What's So Original About Sin?

The Bible says we are all sinners. Everybody is a sinner. No exceptions.

Of course, we want exceptions. More specifically, we want to be the exception. And we think God's pretty uncaring to lay a guilt trip like sin on us.

But it's not about guilt; it's about love. Love willing to point out the barrier that keeps us from the best possible life.

Theologians describe it as "original sin," which means we are born that way. Sin is part of the human condition. We did nothing to cause the condition, and we cannot fix it.

But our sinful nature separates us from God. So God made a way. Since we cannot solve our sin problem, God created a solution for us.

Jesus' death on that terrible cross paid the price for sin. Your sin. My sin. The sins of the world. Although he was as human as we are, he was perfect. Fathered by God's Spirit, he didn't carry our burden of original sin. He was the perfect sacrifice that sin required, and his perfection pays for our imperfection, allowing God's Spirit to start changing our too human nature.

When we choose to make God the Lord of our life (that is, our boss), our sins are charged to Jesus' account and marked "paid in full." And God chooses to forget them. Our slate is wiped clean. Sin's separation is gone.

We have come home.

# WHAT IS THIS THING CALLED PEACE?

*A*s we know Jesus better, his divine power gives us everything we need for living a godly life. He has called us to receive his own glory and goodness! And by that same mighty power, he has given us all of his rich and wonderful promises. He has promised that you will escape the decadence all around you caused by evil desires and that you will share in his divine nature.

- Peter's second letter, chapter 1, verses 3 through 4 (II Pet.1:3-4)
- New Living Translation (NLT)
- Written by Peter, the leader of Jesus' "inner circle," to the churches across Asia Minor, in what is now Turkey. The areas mentioned cover about two thousand square miles. The churches circulated all the letters now recorded in the New Testament, reading them aloud many times in front of each group so the contents could be memorized, a practice of the day.

# What Is This Thing Called Peace?

Charles Wesley lived in the sixteenth century, and during his life, wrote more than 6500 hymns. With all that song-writing, it is a wonder he had time to eat. A greater wonder, though, is the timelessness of his words. A verse in one of his hymns states:

*"He breaks the power of canceled sin.*

*He sets the prisoner free.*

*His blood can make the foulest clean.*

*His blood availed for me."*

The blood this verse refers to is the blood Jesus shed dying for our sins, the sacrifice that created the way we can become whole. He made the gift of real life, salvation, available.

We accept this wonderful gift when we become a child of God. And not only does God's grace cancel our sin, it also breaks sin's power to hold us prisoners. Change is possible.

Anything God calls sin, he gives us the power to conquer. We are not helpless. God offers us enough power to overcome anything that keeps us from his best for us.

Is it magic? No. Is it automatic, without effort? Rarely. There's work to do, decisions to make, difficulties to overcome. It can be tough. But with God's power in us, joining ours, we can be free.

God's power is available to all his children. As much as we can handle. The amount of power we receive from God is roughly equal to our commitment to God.

And, as Wesley wrote, *"'Tis life, and health, and peace."*

# You Guilty Sinner You

> ...the Lord does not see as mortals see; they look on the outward appearance, but the Lord looks on the heart.

- The first book of Samuel, chapter 1, verse 7 (I Sam. 1:7)
- New Revised Standard Version (NRSV)
- This Old Testament book is the history of the Jewish nation at the time it got its first kings, Saul and David. The book starts with the birth of the prophet, Samuel, the person God used to choose the kings.

# You Guilty Sinner You

A few people believe there is no sin in their lives, but most of us know better. It is not a matter of being the worst person in the world, although from day to day we may feel like a contender. But, down deep, everything is not quite "on."

Most of us own a secret closet—things we don't want others to know—so we try to pretend to be somebody we're not. To act as if we're more valuable than we think we are. We believe others wouldn't like us if they really knew us.

We put a lot of energy into this act. We try to fit in wherever we are, whatever it takes. To be all things to all people. Ignoring hurts. Not addressing the evil around us. Making nice. Putting on a happy face. You know the drill. Don't let anybody in because then they'll know.

Then along comes God. He knows all our secrets, sees through all our pretenses. Worst of all, he's fully aware of our sins. All of them. Every single one.

All the carefully draped skeletons in our secret closet are out in the open to God. And we can't dare to believe he could love us.

But he does. Baggage and all. No matter what.

And if we accept his love and love him in return, God teaches us how to love ourselves.

This is news beyond our highest hopes. The great news of a solid foundation for all that life can be.

# Who Qualifies?

*G*od loved the world so much that he gave his one and only Son so that whoever believes in him may not be lost, but have eternal life. God did not send his Son into the world to judge the world guilty, but to save the world through him.

- The gospel written by John, Chapter 3, verses 16 through 17 (John 3:16-17)
- New Century Version (NCV)
- The words of Jesus as recorded by an eyewitness, disciple John. John also wrote three letters (I John - III John) and Revelation, a mystical book prophesying end times, including the end of the age and Jesus' final return.

# Who Qualifies?

Who qualifies for God's forgiveness? To have God's Holy Spirit become part of whom they are? To start down a new path?

Everybody. Yes, everybody. Which makes some folks unhappy.

For some, it is about themselves. Because they want life to stay as it is, they insist their sins are beyond forgiving. If God is willing to forgive them, it takes away some kind of celestial permission to sin, and they have to change. But if they are too bad, even for God, they can avoid change and continue on their way, all the while failing to realize the painful confines of their chosen path.

Some focus on others. They acknowledge their own dainty sins as forgivable, but the sins of others—flat out transgressors—require some heavy-duty repenting to earn forgiveness. And if any forgiveness is given, which in their minds is questionable, it should be conditional.

Most of us, though, are in the middle of that road. We know our lives wouldn't win prizes—especially if everything were out in the open. It's a simple fact—and we somehow know it—that we've missed the mark, which is what "sin" means. Something is missing.

Our question is, "Does God love me enough to forgive me just the way I am?" The answer, resounding through all of history, is "Yes! Yes! Yes!"

Better yet, forgiveness is a gift, not something to be earned. As with all gifts, we need only to accept it.

And, having accepted such a gift, to treasure it.

# The Big Choice

...Jesus told them this story. A man had two sons. The younger son told his father, "I want my share of your estate now, instead of waiting until you die." So his father agreed to divide his wealth between his sons. A few days later this younger son packed all his belongings and took a trip to a distant land, and there he wasted all his money on wild living. About the time his money ran out, a great famine swept over the land, and he began to starve. He persuaded a local farmer to hire him to feed his pigs. The boy became so hungry that even the pods he was feeding the pigs looked good to him. But no one gave him anything. When he finally came to his senses, he said to himself, "At home even the hired men have food enough to spare and here I am, dying of hunger—I will go home to my father and say 'Father, I have sinned against both heaven and you, and I am no longer worthy of being called your son. Please take me on as a hired man.'" So he returned home to his father. And while he was still a long distance away, his father saw him coming. Filled with love and compassion, he ran to his son, embraced and kissed him.

- The gospel written by Luke, chapter 15, verses 11 through 20 (Luke 15:11-20)

- New Living Translation (NLT)

- The words of Jesus in a parable (a teaching story), speaking to a large crowd. Luke was a Greek physician who left his profession to travel and work with Paul.

# The Big Choice

Jesus told about a young man who thought he knew more about life than his father. To get on with life, he demanded an immediate inheritance so he could make his point in the big city.

Receiving it, off he went. Straight into abject failure. He blew his substantial inheritance. He renounced his religion. He lost all the friends his money could buy. He ended up—dirty, hungry, defeated—as a day laborer in a job nobody else wanted. Living with pigs.

One day the son "came to his senses." He realized he had rebelled against love acting for his benefit. He had to go home.

He knew his culture's inhibitions on what he had done. He was as good as dead. His father could not forgive him. He would never again be part of the family. He risked everything, even life itself, by going back, but with the way his life was going, it was a risk he had to take.

As he trudged toward home, filthy, smelling like a pig, his father saw him and, instead of turning his back, ran to meet him. He threw his arms around his son—dirt, stench and all.

The story's father is God. And we, like the son, think we know a better way to live than God does. Who, with regret, come to see how wrong we are. We wonder if we can go home.

The good news is that we can. God is waiting, ready to welcome us when we turn our hearts toward home. It's called Grace—receiving God's favor without earning it.

Notice, though, the father never went after the son. He waited for him.

God is like that. We have a free will. We can live life on our terms or on God's terms. It's forever our choice.

# A Brand New You

*T*here was a man named Nicodemus (nick uh DEEM us) who was one of the Pharisees and an important Jewish leader. One night Nicodemus came to Jesus and said, "Teacher, we know you are a teacher sent from God, because no one can do the miracles you do unless God is with him." Jesus answered, "I tell you the truth, unless one is born again, he cannot be in God's kingdom." Nicodemus said, "But if a person is already old, how can he be born again? He cannot enter his mother's body again. So how can a person be born a second time?" But Jesus answered, "I tell you the truth, unless one is born from water [physical birth] and the Spirit [spiritual birth], he cannot enter God's kingdom. Human life comes from human parents, but spiritual life comes from the Spirit."

- The gospel written by John, chapter 3, verses 1 through 6 (John 3:1-6)

- New Century Version (NCV)

- The words of Jesus to a religious leader who came to Jesus late one night to ask about the life and power Jesus had, but the leader didn't have, despite his education, devotion and position.

> When you read "Jewish leader," think *church* leader. The Jews were God's only church at the time of Christ. Today, there are many churches serving God. So, today might read "Baptist," "Roman Catholic," "Pentecostal," "Methodist," "Presbyterian" or many other church designations.

# A Brand New You

A new baby is often the beginning of the end for the camcorder. And when they're not taping posterity, perfectly literate adults hang over the crib cooing and babbling gibberish. Babies earn rave reviews—and more taping—just by slobbering and burping. Try that as an adult!

As the months go by, phone bills run up as the baby sprouts a tooth, sits up, starts to crawl. Grandma and Grandpa engage in phone conversations with the non-speaking infant.

Finally comes the big day when the baby takes a step. Pandemonium breaks out. Excitement reigns. The camcorder chews through tape and drains its batteries daily. Adults, who walk—and even dance—easily, beam their encouragement at the wonder of the baby's unsteady steps.

When the baby's reeling gait begins to degenerate into a tumble, every adult hand in the room shoots out to cover sharp edges. Tears get soothed. The encouragement level cranks up.

It's a wonderful time.

And so it is when we are born spiritually. Jesus called it "born again." Your physical birth is not your decision. Your spiritual birth is.

When you decide you want to turn your life around—that is, repent—the Bible says the angels in heaven celebrate. As you take faltering steps toward God, he cheers encouragement and runs to you.

God celebrates your spiritual birth even more than the happiest of parents celebrate a physical birth. And all of heaven applauds you, the newest baby.

# What Makes the Difference?

*I*n telling you about these gifts we have even used the very words given to us by the Holy Spirit, not words that we as men might choose. So we use the Holy Spirit's words to explain the Holy Spirit's facts. But the man who isn't a Christian can't understand and can't accept these thoughts from God, which the Holy Spirit teaches us. They sound foolish to him because only those who have the Holy Spirit within them can understand what the Holy Spirit means. Others just can't take it in. But the spiritual man has insight into everything, and that bothers and baffles the man of the world, who can't understand him at all. How could he? For certainly he has never been one to know the Lord's thoughts, or to discuss them with him, or to move the hands of God in prayer. But, strange as it seems, we Christians actually do have within us a portion of the very thoughts and mind of Christ.

- Paul's first letter to Corinth, chapter 2, verses 13 through 16 (I Cor. 2:13-16)
- The Living Bible (TLB)
- Paul was constantly amazed that the presence of the Holy Spirit in his life allowed him to even glimpse God's thoughts, let alone think them, and gave him the power to accomplish God's destiny for him. The book of Acts contains a historic record of Paul's travels and work.

# What Makes the Difference?

Our life turns upside down and around when we become God's child because it makes us a whole new person. We are born again as a new being. Our physical birth made us a new being. Our spiritual birth does, too.

At the moment of our rebirth, God's Spirit comes to live in us. That's right. God himself moves in. That's what makes the change so huge. His Spirit and our spirit become one.

Nobody can explain it, and it seems beyond belief that God would do such a thing. So some say it can't happen, that it doesn't happen.

But we can't explain a lot of things. We can't, for instance, explain human love. But who, besides an eleven-year-old boy revolted at the thought, would say love can't happen, doesn't happen? Deny it, theorize about it, rhapsodize on it, do whatever you want with it, but the fact is people keep changing their lives forever by falling in love.

And so it is when we fall in love with God. Our lives change forever. Because God gives us himself. The reality is not in understanding it, but in experiencing it.

God's Spirit becomes a part of each child of God. To guide us, teach us, inspire us, give us courage, warn us and, when necessary, close doors in our face. He does whatever it takes to help us grow to be more and more like Jesus, our ultimate goal.

*The automobile was supposed to solve the pollution problem, and television was supposed to improve the culture. Given that history, why do we still think we can predict future consequences?*

# First You Walk

*But to all who received him [Jesus Christ], he gave the right to become children of God. All they needed to do was to trust him to save them. All those who believe this are reborn!—not a physical rebirth resulting from human passion or plan—but from the will of God.*

- The gospel written by John, chapter 1, verses 12 through 13 (John 1:12-13)
- The Living Bible (TLB)
- "Gospel" means good news. Part of the good news for John, who started out known for his temper, was that he ended up known as the apostle of love.

# First You Walk

Our spiritual birth gives us a fresh new start. The Bible says we become new people. The change is huge. Life is different.

Because our bodies are grown, we can miss the idea that we are actually babies, spiritual babies. Which fact can be a tad disconcerting. We expect to automatically be as competent in our new spiritual life as we have become in our adult physical life.

A lot of people get stuck right there. They think that what happens on the day of their spiritual birth is all that will happen. That their first step is as good as it gets.

But there's a whole lot of growing to do to get to the best places.

Each day, we tell God we want to do what he wants us to do. To be what he wants us to be. To say what he wants us to say. And, with his help, we set out.

This is how we learn to walk spiritually. We learn to walk the walk, not just talk the talk.

Like a baby, we will stumble some days. Just as an occasional tumble doesn't make a baby a guilty failure, a spiritual misstep isn't the end of our spiritual walk, either.

Finally, like the baby, we learn to walk well. Then run. Hop. Skip. Jump. We enjoy our new life, look forward to tomorrow and dream of what we might become when we grow up.

# Celebrating What Is

*D*ear brothers and sisters, when I was with you I couldn't talk to you as I would to mature Christians. I had to talk as though you belonged to this world or as though you were infants in the Christian life. I had to feed you with milk and not with solid food, because you couldn't handle anything stronger. And you still aren't ready.

- First Corinthians (kore IN thee unz), chapter three, verses 1 through 2 (I Cor. 3:1-2)
- New Living Translation (NLT)
- Paul's first letter to the church at Corinth. Paul's letters to Corinth consist mostly of advice in resolving problems. Paul gives biblical reasons for his advice to this very diverse group of people (all ages, all economic groups, all education levels, all races, from all types of backgrounds, etc.) on how to get along with each other.

# Celebrating What Is

We celebrate when a baby is born. What potential! What hope! What plans we have for this new life.

If the baby can't meet our expectations, joy turns to mourning. We had such dreams for all that would be, all that could be, in the baby's life. And now we must put those dreams aside.

Our baby is handicapped. Limited in what can ever be achieved. And so we struggle to celebrate what is and move beyond what might have been.

A heart of love can grow the strength to celebrate whatever reality is. Every baby gives us the potential to become more than we were before the baby's birth.

We, of course, can't always see it that way. At least, not at first. We reason that our hopes and dreams weren't too lofty and grand. Why were we denied them? We focus on lost dreams and never see the little, damaged baby, fighting like an Amazon, willing to love even our broken hearts.

Celebrating life in these circumstances is painful.

Perhaps equally distressing, though, are healthy, capable children who refuse to grow up and never accept responsibility for their actions.

Can you understand, then, how God mourns when his children choose not to grow, preferring to remain spiritual infants?

A baby unable to grow is sad, but the new life still draws us to love and growth. Being unwilling to grow is a tragedy, ending only in frustration and feelings of inadequacy.

# MOVING PAST THE RULE PILE

*A*nd God spoke all these words, saying:
"I am the Lord your God…You shall have no other gods before Me. You will not make for yourself a carved image— any likeness of anything that is in heaven above, or that is in the earth beneath, or that is in the water under the earth; you will not bow down to them nor serve them…

"You will not take the name of the Lord your God in vain, for the Lord will not hold him guiltless who takes His name in vain.

"Remember the Sabbath day, to keep it holy. Six days you shall labor and do all your work, but the seventh day is the Sabbath of the Lord your God…

"Honor your father and mother, that your days may be long upon the land…

"You shall not murder.

"You shall not commit adultery.

"You shall not steal.

"You shall not bear false witness against your neighbor.

"You shall not covet your neighbor's house…wife…or servants…or [animals], nor anything that is your neighbor's."

**The Ten Commandments**
- Exodus (X uh duss), chapter 20, verses 1 through 17 (Ex. 20:1-17)

- New King James Version (NKJV)

- Moses, who led God's people out of slavery in Egypt, wrote Exodus. The classic motion picture *Exodus* is based on this book of the Bible. The act of Moses receiving the stone tablets on which God recorded his commandments is one of the book's highlights.

# Moving Past the Rule Pile

In each new situation we encounter, we have to learn how things work, the rules, so to speak. And so it is with becoming a new Christian.

The Bible has rules for victorious living, such as the Ten Commandments. The church throws in a few. Parents add their say, too. Heap on the rules learned through experience, and the rule pile becomes huge, not to mention intimidating.

What do we do with a mountain of rules? Where do we start? The easiest thing to do is to conditionally accept every rule in the pile. For now.

And so we start—with a bundle of rules and a hope they will some day make sense.

As we investigate what we got ourselves into, we learn what God says in the Bible. We start to understand how his words apply. All the while, God's Holy Spirit guides, teaches and grows us. Ideas and understanding take shape. Wisdom, if you will. We build a framework in which the rules fit. We discard mistaken, inappropriate rules that don't fit our new knowledge. The rule pile shrinks.

God's rules are always our foundation, but no life can be fully defined by rules, so God moves us beyond them. We grow past the dos and don'ts into our birthright of peace and joy—and the sure knowledge we are loved.

Rules can only be a beginning. Making them the entire Christian experience stunts our growth and misses the best parts.

# OBVIOUSLY, RULES ARE NOT ENOUGH

> You foolish Galatians! Who put a spell on you? Before your very eyes you had a clear description of the death of Jesus Christ on the cross! Tell me this one thing: did you receive God's Spirit by doing what the Law requires or by hearing the gospel and believing it? How can you be so foolish! You began by God's Spirit; do you now want to finish by your own power?

- Galations (guh LAY shunz), chapter 3, verses 1 through 3 (Gal. 3:1-3)
- Today's English Version (TEV)
- Paul's letter to the church in Galatia (guh LAY sha). Paul founded the church in Galatia. After he left, other leaders came telling the people to go back to their old, failed ways. Paul is obviously unhappy in this letter.

# Obviously Rules Are Not Enough

Magazines often have articles with rules for having a happy marriage. Or raising wonderful children. Or managing your career. Or some such.

Sometimes the rules fit. For the most part, though, you wonder what planet the writer comes from. Your spouse isn't the charmingly accommodative pushover of the article. Your children certainly missed the part about the wonderful adventure of sampling new cuisines, not to mention the fun of picking up. And your boss? Please.

Religious rules can be like that, too. They establish concepts, but they don't cover the amazing variety of personalities and situations that make up our lives.

Plus, rules fit what went before, and God is always doing something new. He creates unique people. No copies, all originals. And times change. It would help if everybody entered the world clutching instruction books specific to their life and times—all answers nicely indexed.

Well, it turns out there is an instruction book, the Bible. And for times when we don't quite see how it applies, there's a teacher, too: God's Spirit in us, walking where we walk, not only accustomed to our uniqueness but the author of it.

We should spend time with the instruction book daily, plus additional time communicating with God. These things tune our hearts to recognize and hear his voice, and bypassing them makes us spiritually hard of hearing.

# Hearing God's Voice

*T*he Spirit shows what is true and will come and guide you into the full truth. The Spirit does not speak on his own. He will tell you only what he has heard from me, and he will let you know what is going to happen. The Spirit will bring glory to me by taking my message and telling it to you.

- The gospel written by disciple John, chapter 16, verses 13 through 14 (John 16:13)

- The International Student Bible for Catholics - *New Testament Edition* (CEV)

  The Contemporary English Version of the Bible has the same text in both Protestant and Catholic editions. What differs, slightly, are the added explanatory articles.

- The words of Jesus, teaching his disciples about what will happen after his death. Matthew, Mark and Luke wrote the gospels bearing their names chronologically while John wrote his gospel by topic.

# Hearing God's Voice

How do we know what God wants us to do? How does this work? Truth is, we have to learn to hear God's voice.

Voices? We're supposed to hear voices?

Well, sort of. We need to hear God's voice, but it is rarely an actual, out-loud voice. Almost never, in fact.

Here's how it works. God now lives in us, is part of us. His Spirit unites with ours to teach and guide us. Through this union, God speaks to us.

We already have an idea of how this works from experiencing pangs of conscience when our own spirit speaks to us. In a similar way, God's Spirit speaks to us. We have ideas that are not ours, and they feel right. We know things we have no way of knowing. We recognize God's hand in creating coincidences. Sometimes a thought won't let us go. And so on.

It sounds simple and pleasant. But Jesus used the word *dunamis* to describe the power we receive this way. *Dunamis* means dynamite. Don't expect bland.

Like the conscience, we can stifle God's Spirit by not recognizing his presence or by refusing to listen. This is a real danger because it leaves us to our own devices, and we end up ineffective, frustrated and testy.

Letting this power fill us, on the other hand, moves us beyond ourselves so we can accomplish all we were created to do. We're blessed people who hear one special voice.

*If you won't start from where you are,  
you can't start at all.*

# UNGAMES

*I* know very well how foolish it sounds to those who are lost, when they hear that Jesus died to save them. But we who are saved recognize this message as the very power of God.

- Paul's first letter to the church at Corinth, chapter 1, verse 18 (I Cor. 1:18)
- The Living Bible (TLB)
- The Corinthian church had many problems and conflicts, but, eventually—and it was one really long "eventually"—the people grew into what they were called to be because they allowed the Holy Spirit to change them.

# Ungames

Christians live life facing God. Non-Christians live life facing away from God. Obviously, they see things differently.

And Christians speak of communicating with God. Such talk is not well received, even viewed as a game of one-upmanship. Arrogance, in fact.

But Christianity is not one-upmanship. It is not a game of "God loves me best." It's just that when God is at the center of a life, that life is very different. While the difference can look like self-importance, it's really just a difference in focus where the goal is responding to God's Spirit in us.

To people who haven't experienced God's presence integrated into their lives, this sounds ridiculous. Somewhere beyond unbelievable, in fact. A scam.

But the Christian life absolutely requires God's constant presence. We can't accomplish God's plans without it. His Spirit guides our thoughts and allows us, amazingly, to experience God's thoughts. This is how we move beyond ourselves. Otherwise, we only have willpower to do the heavy lifting, and anybody who's ever been on a diet can tell you how well that works.

Sometimes we follow God's guidance well. Sometimes not so well. But the more we follow God, the better we get at it. And the better we get at it, the more we can accomplish what God put us on earth to do.

The Christian life, then, is not us doing what we think we can do. It is God working in and through us to do what he wants us to do.

Rather than arrogance, it is a humble attempt to be God's person.

# Learning to Hear

*I*f you love me, you will obey my commands. I will ask the Father, and he will give you another Helper to be with you forever—the Spirit of truth. The world cannot accept him, because it does not see him or know him. But you know him, because he lives with you and he will be in you. I will not leave you all alone like orphans; I will come back to you. In a little while the world will not see me anymore, but you will see me. Because I live, you will live, too. On that day you will know that I am in my Father, and that you are in me and I am in you. Those who know my commands and obey them are the ones who love me, and my Father will love those who love me. I will love them and will show myself to them.

- The gospel written by John, chapter 14, verses 15 through 21 (John 14:15-21)

- New Century Version (NCV)

- The words of Jesus instructing his twelve closest disciples, including John, about his coming death and the subsequent gift of the Holy Spirit, which meant they wouldn't be all alone like orphans. None of the disciples had a clue what Jesus meant until they suddenly experienced it about fifty days later.

# Learning to Hear

God speaks both to the world as a whole and to individuals. God speaks universally in the Bible. As we become conversant with what the Bible says, God speaks to us through its words.

This means, of course, to hear God's voice correctly, we need to know the Bible, his word to us. This takes study. Not casual, occasional reading but study. And, through that, letting God's Spirit teach us.

The Bible is not the easiest book in the world to fathom. It originated in different languages, differing cultures, through long centuries. Plus, the Bible contains God's thoughts, which are so unlike our own, and take some stretching to comprehend.

Without a solid Biblical foundation, though, we get off track. We may decide we hear God's voice, when it is actually our pride. Or a matter of convenience. Or our own desires and fears. The Bible teaches us how to separate out the noise.

When God speaks, he never contradicts the Bible. Obviously. Since the Bible is God's word, God would be contradicting himself. This means anything God says will be consistent with the Bible—which, in turn, is consistent within itself.

This fact is our foundation, our protection. We may think new thoughts or hear new ideas that seem good, but if they contradict God, we are hearing the wrong stuff. It is God's voice, and his voice alone, that keeps us on the right track.

# GROWING UP IS GOOD TO DO

*B*ut the Spirit produces the fruit of love, joy, peace, patience, kindness, goodness, faithfulness, gentleness, self-control. There is no law that says these things are wrong.

- Galatians (guh LAY shunz), chapter 5, verses 22 through 23 (Gal. 5:22-23)
- New Century Version (NCV)
- Paul's letter to the church at Galatia (guh LAY sha) describing the results of depending on God's Holy Spirit

*T*ake care to live in me, and let me live in you. For a branch can't produce fruit when severed from the vine. Nor can you be fruitful apart from me. Yes, I am the vine; you are the branches. Whoever lives in me and I in him shall produce a large crop of fruit. For apart from me you can't do a thing.

- The gospel written by John, chapter 15, verses 4 through 5 (John 15:4-5)
- The Living Bible (TLB)
- The words of Jesus about where we find our power

# Growing Up Is Good To Do

We grow up in stages. We start as babies, become toddlers, then kids, pre-teens, teenagers, young adults and finally, hopefully, mature adults.

Physical growth just happens. Emotional growth, though, takes intentional effort. With some people, bodies age, but, alas, maturity never arrives. Teen-age angst becomes a way of life. They remain perpetually selfish, self-focused, moody and drifting. By choice. Amazingly, they believe aimless drifting is as good as life gets.

Some Christians don't grow up either. Not realizing it is a relationship and not a religion, not understanding God lives in them ready to give them strength and wisdom, they get just enough religion to make themselves miserable. Trying to will themselves to be all the Bible says they should be keeps them testy and spiritually stunted. Pity.

There's good stuff in spiritual maturity. It takes work, intentional effort like prayer, Bible study, responding to God's guidance and being part of a Christian community, but the payoff is worth far more than the effort. In the Bible, Paul talks about the fruit, the results, of God's Spirit in us—the payoff—as " love, joy, peace, patience, kindness, goodness, faithfulness, gentleness and self-control." Everything that makes life sing.

Just as fruit develops from its attachment to the tree, so we grow by being "attached" to God. We do the intentional part, and the rest, like fruit on a tree, just happens.

Growth may take more time than our impatient selves appreciate, but growing up is very, very good to do.

# WORKING THE PLAN

*A*thletes work hard to win a crown that cannot last, but we do it for a crown that will last forever. I don't run without a goal. And I don't box by beating my fists in the air.

- First Corinthians (kore IN thee unz), Chapter 9, Verses 13 through 14 (I Cor. 9:13-14)
- The International Student Bible for Catholics - *New Testament Edition* (CEV)
- In his first letter to the church at Corinth, Paul writes about one of the reasons a life of faith is worth the effort. Paul uses a lot of sports analogies in his writings.

# Working the Plan

What does it mean to be a Christian? If I make God my lifetime boss, what can I expect? What happens?

Now these are valid questions, expected questions. But tough to answer because God doesn't work with a cookie cutter. God is about the new and the different.

God's plan for your life is just that: a plan for *your* life, nobody else's. All the plans for all the lives weave together in a giant, glorious tapestry, but each is unique.

Let's look at some facts.

The personality you were born with is the personality God intended you to have. If you're noisy, that's the plan. If you're quiet, that's the plan. We're not talking about short fuses, abusive language and the like. That's what you added, and it's time to knock it off. With God's help, of course.:)

If you're happy in the job you have, it's probably where God wants you to be. You get an unsettled feeling when you're somewhere God doesn't want you to be, doing what God doesn't want you to do. If you sincerely want to walk with God, he'll sincerely let you know when you need to make a change.

Meanwhile you walk it out a day at a time. It's called living by faith—a daily trust that God will show up. We don't get five-year-plans from above, only a daily adventure.

And God leads where we never dreamed of going.

# Does Morality Count?

With the Lord's authority let me say this: Live no longer as the ungodly do, for they are hopelessly confused. Their closed minds are full of darkness, they are far away from the life of God because they have shut their minds and hardened their hearts against him. They don't care any more about right and wrong, and they have given themselves over to immoral ways. Their lives are filled with all kinds of impurity and greed. But that isn't what you were taught when you learned about Christ. Since you have heard all about him and have learned the truth that is in Jesus, throw off your old evil nature and your former way of life, which is rotten through and through, full of lust and deception. Instead, there must be a spiritual renewal of your thoughts and attitudes. You must display a new nature because you are a new person, created in God's likeness—righteous, holy, and true.

- Ephesians (ee FEE zhunz), chapter 4, verses 17 through 24 (Eph. 4:17-24)

- New Living Translation (NLT)

- Paul's letter to the church at Ephesus (F uh suss), one of the churches he founded. Two of his beloved co-workers, Priscilla, thought to be the daughter of a Roman Senator, and her husband, Aquila, were instrumental in the growth and strength of the Ephesian church.

# Does Morality Count?

A moral person may not choose to be a Christian, but a Christian can't choose to be an immoral person and stay connected to Christ. Morality is a necessary, integral part of the Christian life.

If God is our boss—our Lord—and the Bible is his word, it follows that the Bible lays out the benchmarks for living.

The Bible states clearly what is acceptable to God and what is not. The Ten Commandments are not, as the saying goes, the Ten Suggestions. And we read about more moral standards, variations on the original theme, throughout the Bible.

These standards apply throughout the ages, as current as today's newspaper. We ignore the Bible at the cost of diminishing our lives.

Moral standards are not killjoy instructions from a God with pursed lips and a bad attitude. Quite the contrary. They are clear instructions from a loving father about how to get the best from life—and avoid a lot of pain in the process.

We may think we know better. We may choose to break God's law. But we end up broken by choices that ignore God's will—God's best—for our lives.

The Bible's rules are the bedrock. God's Spirit living in us moves us above and beyond mere rules to the sweet stratosphere of daily communion with God.

But the Bible is where we start.

# WALKING TALKS MORE THAN TALKING WALKS

*For the Kingdom of God is not just fancy talk; it is living by God's power.*

- First Corinthians (kore IN thee unz), chapter 4, verse 20 (I Cor. 4:20)
- New Living Translation (NLT)
- Paul's first letter to the church at Corinth. Some of the members thought talking the faith was enough. Some things do not change.

# Walking Talks More Than Talking Walks

Talking a good game is different from playing a good game. Talking's easy, while playing a good game takes practice. Hard, long hours of practice.

Some people would just as soon not bother with the practicing part. They prefer strutting, puffing and talking about their supposed prowess to getting sweaty and actually acquiring any. So we have clubhouse golfers, bleacher baseball players and couch potato quarterbacks. All pretty harmless.

Christianity's another area where walking takes more effort than talking. As usual, the talking's easy. Walking it out involves daily effort and commitment.

And, unfortunately, talk-only Christians are not harmless. They get the jargon down pat, then use it to excuse inexcusable behavior. Their walk reflects none of the love that should be the Christian's hallmark. All-talk, no-walk Christians cause a lot of pain.

Worse yet, they turn people away from the joy and wonder of a relationship with God. Talkers distort the reality of God. People who are hurting and in search of God's love are turned off, pushed away from the very thing they seek. God's true nature is too disguised to recognize.

Some of these talkers are evil, using God's name to perfume their hidden agendas. Most are simply uninformed and misguided, doing life by the numbers. They never learned that Christianity is a relationship, not a do-it-yourself, feel-superior philosophy.

Ignore any bad-will ambassadors you run into. Don't let their attitudes, words or actions keep you from claiming the walk of a lifetime.

# WHERE'S THE POWER?

After this manner therefore pray ye: Our Father which art in heaven, Hallowed be thy name. Thy kingdom come. Thy will be done in earth, as it is in heaven. Give us this day our daily bread. And forgive us our debts, as we forgive our debtors. And lead us not into temptation, but deliver us from evil; For thine is the kingdom, and the power, and the glory, for ever. Amen.

**The Lord's Prayer**
- The Gospel written by Matthew, Chapter 6, Verses 9 through 13 (Matt. 6:9-13)
- King James Version (KJV)
- The words of Jesus giving his disciples a pattern for prayer. One of Jesus' inner circle of twelve disciples, Matthew had been a tax collector—and probably as much a crook as all the other tax collectors of the time.

# Where's the Power?

Prayer is conversation with our father. Form doesn't matter. Time of day, place, posture or the words you use are unimportant. You simply have a regular conversation with God—as you would with anybody you loved. We learn to recognize God's voice and get power beyond our own through prayer.

Like all conversations, prayer is two-sided. If, for example, you call your parents to say you love them and list the things you want, then hang up without giving them a chance to respond, that's a monologue, not a conversation.

And so it is with prayer. God has things to tell you. Things to help you and prepare you for whatever tomorrow holds.

Here's how it goes. You focus solely on your prayer, think your thoughts, open your mind to his and keep the conversation going until God fills your mind and spirit with enough information to settle things. Old time prayer warriors call it "praying through."

This sounds strange at first. Feels strange, too. Consequently, prayer is often reduced to an occasional drive-by shout at God, better than nothing, but not really prayer that begets power.

Without prayer, you'll sense a lack. A feeling that, regardless of what the Bible promises, you're in this life alone. Perhaps you'll settle for this half-life instead of all that's available to you.

But if you persevere, prayer becomes more natural. Which is good because the fact is that whenever, wherever and however, prayer is our power source.

*If you go through life looking out for #1,
don't expect a crowd at your funeral.*

# The Hold of Habits

*I* don't understand myself at all, for I really want to do what is right, but I don't do it. Instead, I do the very thing I hate. I know perfectly well that what I am doing is wrong, and my bad conscience shows that I agree that the law is good. But I can't help myself, because it is sin inside me that makes me do these evil things. Oh, what a miserable person I am! Who will free me from this life that is dominated by sin?

- Romans, chapter 7, verses 15 through 17 and verse 24 (Rom. 7:15-17, 24)
- New Living Translation (NLT)
- Paul's letter to the church at Rome, speaking of trying to be a Christian through willpower and self-help alone, without the added power of God's Holy Spirit

# The Hold of Habits

Habits are hard to break. Practiced long enough, they become the lifestyle around which we structure our life.

Negative habits produce a lifestyle of sin, one that keeps us from experiencing all God has for us. And sin can grip us like steel. Thoughts of change could daunt Superman.

After all, if losing ten pounds is a struggle, where in the world are we going to get enough willpower to break the habits of a lifetime? How can we possibly live a life that makes God smile?

Fortunately, we don't have to produce all the power we need to break free. It's not a matter of willpower alone. Sure, effort is required, but so is letting God's power work through us to provide the necessary strength beyond our own.

There is an old saying, "Let go and let God." Let go of the problem. Give it to God and let God provide the strength, wisdom and guidance we need.

It sounds wonderful. It is wonderful. But for most of us, letting go is hard to do, so we struggle on alone. We don't take time to be with God. To listen for his voice, his guidance. To allow God to work through us. We're too accustomed to going it alone, and we need to learn to fight temptation with prayer.

God is on our side. He wants the best for us. He'll give us the power to do what we can't do alone, but we have to let him in.

# How Far Do You Want To Go?

So now there is no condemnation for those who belong to Christ Jesus. For the power of the life-giving Spirit has freed you through Christ Jesus from the power of sin that leads to death. The law of Moses could not save us, because of our sinful nature. But God put into effect a different plan to save us. He sent his own Son in a human body like ours, except that ours are sinful. God destroyed sin's control over us by giving his Son as a sacrifice for our sins. Those who are dominated by the sinful nature think about sinful things, but those who are controlled by the Holy Spirit think about things that please the Spirit. If your sinful nature controls your mind, there is death. But if the Holy Spirit controls your mind, there is life and peace.

- Romans, chapter 8, verses 1 through 3 and verses 5-6 (Rom. 8:1-3, 5-6)
- New Living Translation (NLT)
- Paul's letter to the church at Rome explaining how God's Holy Spirit goes beyond our willpower and self-help to give us victory over sin and death.

# How Far Do You Want To Go?

God's power can conquer every sin, every single one of them, regardless of the hold it has over our lives or how large an obstacle it presents to us.

We're the ones who draw lines beyond which, we decide, God is helpless. Sadly, we often draw those lines pretty close in. We don't think even God can get us out of the ditch we got ourselves into. But we're beyond God's reach only if we choose to be.

Some people, frankly, don't want God's help. They'd rather live without a relationship with God than to allow God to erase their desire for things that prevent one.

Most of us, though, want a relationship with God. We want to live in the embrace of God's love, to be and have all God offers. And we try and try to make abundant life happen, but we can't get the job done.

Meanwhile, the power we need is right there—God's Spirit living in us. Recognizing this reality is the first step to tapping into it.

Of course, once we know, we expect immediate results. Sometimes it happens that way. But most times results take time and effort, even struggle.

We prefer an easy path. God chooses the best path. But, whether instantly or after working some stuff out, sin's power over us will be broken.

Nothing is too big for God. We just need to access his power—as long and as often as it takes.

# A Modern Day Tale

*T*rust in the Lord with all thine heart, and lean not unto thine own understanding. In all thy ways acknowledge him, and he shall direct thy paths.

- Proverbs, chapter 3, verses 5 through 6 (Prov. 3:5-6)
- King James Version (KJV)
- Proverbs is King Solomon's book of wisdom. It contains one pithy saying after another, best read in small sections to prevent brain overload. Solomon was ancient Israel's third king, the second son of the more famous King David and his wife, Bathsheba.

# A Modern Day Tale

A young man decided to become a follower of Jesus Christ, to enter into a love relationship with eternal God.

To show God his serious intentions, he sat down to write a list of all the things he was willing to do to serve and honor God.

He worked on his list for days. He ended up with several pages of the many things he was willing to do.

Finally finished, he handed his list to God. God smiled, but refused the list.

So the young man sat down to revise the list. To expand it with every possible thing he could think of to please and glorify God.

Again he handed the list to God. And, again, God smiled, but refused it.

Disappointed, the young man sat down once more to work on the list. But he couldn't think of a thing to add. He thought for days, but he could not manage a single new idea.

Not knowing what God wanted, the young man changed his approach. He took a blank piece of paper and just signed his name at the bottom.

He tentatively handed the blank page to God. God accepted it with a smile.

Which makes sense. God knows the future, we don't. God knows his plan for our lives, we don't.

But blank pages are scary if you don't trust the one filling in the blanks.

# Strong Fingernails

> Now glory be to God, who by his mighty power at work within us is able to do far more than we would ever dare to ask or even dream of—infinitely beyond our highest prayers, desires, thoughts, or hopes.

- Ephesians (ee FEE zhunz), chapter 3, verse 20 (Eph. 3:20)
- The Living Bible (TLB)
- Paul's letter to the church he founded in Ephesus (F uh suss), on the west coast of what is now Turkey, on the Aegean Sea.

## Strong Fingernails

Being a Christian doesn't solve all of life's problems. It's not a cocoon to protect us from life's rough patches or a hermetically sealed bubble to keep us untouched by pain.

Contrary to the hopes of many, God never promises an easy life. He promises to be with us through the thick and thin of life. This doesn't seem like much of a promise—until you experience it.

Remember, God describes himself as a father, and he knows that fathers who make all the decisions for their children and protect them from everything and everybody, handicap their children for life. God chooses the more difficult task of allowing his children freedom.

We have freedom to make mistakes. Freedom to gather emotional and physical scars. Freedom to make decisions with unfortunate consequences. This may seem like the hard way to do life, but it's the tough times that grow us, and it's a mature faith that reaches the heights.

In the middle of tough times, though, things can look depressingly grim. Desert in front us. Desert behind us. Not an oasis in sight.

Our awareness that God is with us keeps us going. His presence supplies hope. We know whatever tomorrow brings, God will be there. Our optimism may take on a ragged edge from time to time, perhaps hide behind a cloud momentarily, but it never abandons us.

So, when we're hanging on by our fingernails, we should pray for strong fingernails. And remember we're not fighting the storm alone.

# WHO LEADS AND WHO FOLLOWS?

To have faith is to be sure of the things we hope for, to be certain of the things we cannot see. It was by their faith that people of ancient times won God's approval.

- Hebrews, chapter 11, verse 1 (Heb. 11:1)
- Today's English Version (TEV)
- The author of this letter is uncertain, although many believe it was Paul's co-worker, Priscilla. Hebrews weaves together themes and concepts from the Old and New Testaments.

And now—all glory to him who alone is God, who saves us through Jesus Christ our Lord; yes, splendor and majesty, all power and authority are his from the beginning; his they are and his they evermore shall be. And he is able to keep you from slipping and falling away, and to bring you, sinless and perfect, into his glorious presence with mighty shouts of everlasting joy.

- Jude, verses 24 through 25 (Ju. 24-25). Jude has only one chapter.
- The Living Bible (TLB)
- Jude, the half-brother of Jesus, wrote this letter to be circulated among all the churches.

# Who Leads and Who Follows?

Christians live by faith. Faith is trusting God enough to follow even when we don't know where he is leading us. Even before we know the question, the answer should be, "Yes, Lord." And God unnerves us by not thinking like a human, while we want things to make sense before we act.

Children do faith well. It is how they live their lives. Mother says they are going to the store, and it doesn't matter that the child doesn't know where the store is or how to get there. Mom does, so off they go.

Adults, though, struggle for some kind of control. Where is the store? Why are we going? How long will it take? Do we have to go now?

What we really want is terra firma. A five-year plan. Or, perhaps a short, explanatory note. Something, anything, to add a smidgeon of certainty. Usually, though, God gives just enough direction for the next step.

Walking by faith takes a lot of, well, faith. There's just something in us that wants to know, ahead of time, how everything's going to turn out.

Because we can't see the entire plan, we may get disoriented in difficult times. Just when we should focus all the more on God, we focus instead on our difficulties, creating delays.

Fortunately, God is patient. He wants our success even more than we do. He'll always lead us to where we need to be, even when we slow things down with detours into doubt.

# No Fence To Sit On

*A*nyone who is not for me is against me; if he isn't helping me, he is hurting my cause.

- The gospel written by Luke, chapter 11, verse 23 (Luke 11:23)
- The Living Bible (TLB)
- The words of Jesus as reported by Luke, a Greek physician and a co-worker/co-traveler with Paul. Luke also wrote the book, Acts of the Apostles, usually called, simply, Acts.

# No Fence To Sit On

Taking sides makes people unhappy, so fence-sitting becomes popular, a risk-free way to do life.

Christianity, though, doesn't have a fence to sit on. It requires choice. The Bible says, "Choose this day whom you will serve."

Many people, even church people, have a problem with this. We like no-risk fences. We want our comfortable, fanny-shaped fences that save us from social faux pas.

But there's no fence. Which is good when you think about it. Fence-sitting doesn't lead to progress, while choices move life along. Avoiding necessary choices takes us in toxic directions.

Our choice about God may be simply neglecting to make a choice. Sin is the default of refusing, or neglecting, to choose God. We either live in God, or we live in sin, away from God.

When we live in sin, our words and actions reveal our address. We may be good citizens, but we focus our hearts only on do-it-yourself goals—money, power, status, whatever—and don't include God. Our life is all about us. The present is dissatisfaction, and the end is death.

When we live in Christ, our words and actions reveal our address, too. Our goal is to be God's person and follow him—which may incidentally lead to money, power, status, whatever, that being up to God. Our life is about God. The present is joy; the end is life.

We need to choose. There's no fence. We might as well quit looking and decide where we're going to live.

# Why Bother?

If you believe that Jesus is the Christ—that he is God's Son and your Savior—then you are a child of God. And all who love the Father love his children, too. So you can find out how much you love God's children—your brothers and sisters in the Lord—by how much you love and obey God. Loving God means doing what he tells us to do, and really, that isn't hard at all; for every child of God can obey him, defeating sin and evil pleasure by trusting Christ to help him. But who could possibly fight and win this battle except by believing that Jesus is truly the Son of God?

- Disciple John's first letter, chapter 5, verses 1 through 5 (I Jn. 5:1-5)
- The Living Bible (TLB)
- John's letters were written in his later years when he was the only living disciple. Exiled to Patmos, he was the only disciple not martyred for his faith.

# Why Bother?

If being a Christian doesn't guarantee a problem-free life, why bother? Why turn life upside down if nothing changes?

But life does change. Oh, indeedy.

Now, whatever we do, wherever we are, whatever the time, we're never alone. Good days, bad days: Never alone. Even in truly foul days, we know God won't let us drop all the way to the bottom of the well.

And we have joy. Tears may streak our cheeks, but still there's joy. Burdens may buckle our knees, but hope bubbles up through the pain. Peace, unbidden, seeps into our hearts.

Skeptics scoff at this kind of talk, say it's like whistling in a graveyard to keep our courage up. No more than happy talk to reassure ourselves. A matter, they say, of forced cheerfulness and unrealistic thinking.

But anybody who's walked through valleys of tears with God, leaning hard to keep from falling, knows it's real. Our dependable God gives muscular care.

God promises he won't let life go beyond what we can handle. It's not about easy; he has a very high regard for our handling capacity—but he keeps us from plummeting over the edge, every day for all of life.

As good as that is, and maybe better, when this life is finished, he welcomes us into Heaven to spend eternity in the very presence of his love. This life is only a moment in time, a snap of the fingers. The reward for what we do with it lasts forever.

*Walking with God means you have the
biggest guy on your side.*

# Big Ideas, Weak Knees

Lord, you have examined me and know all about me.
You know when I sit down and when I get up.
You know my thoughts before I think them.
You know where I go and where I lie down.
You know thoroughly everything I do.
Lord, even before I say a word, you already know it.
You are all around me—in front and in back—and have put your hand on me.
Your knowledge is amazing to me; it is more than I can understand.
Where can I go to get away from your Spirit?
Where can I run from you?
If I go up to the heavens, you are there.
If I lie down in the grave, you are there.
If I rise with the sun in the east and settle in the west beyond the sea,
Even there you would guide me.
With your right hand you would hold me.
I could say, "The darkness will hide me, Let the light around me turn into night."
But even the darkness is not dark to you.
The night is as light as the day; darkness and light are the same to you.
You made my whole being; you formed me in my mother's body.
I praise you because you made me in an amazing and wonderful way.
What you have done is wonderful.
I know this very well.
You saw my bones being formed as I took shape in my mother's body.
When I was put together there, you saw my body as it was formed.
All the days planned for me were written in your book before I was one day old.
God, your thoughts are precious to me.
There are so many!
If I could count them, they would be more than all the grains of sand.
When I wake up, I am still with you.

- The Psalms (silent P, rhymes with palms), chapter 139, verses 1 through 18

- New Century Version (NCV)

- Written by ancient Israel's King David, expressing joy and amazement about God's love and care

# Big Ideas, Weak Knees

God's in the stretching business—and we're the objects of his efforts. Not the standstill sort, he intends to move us right along, our full comprehension not being required.

As an instance, God called Moses to free his people from Egypt, and a scared-silly Moses told God he had the wrong man. Moses explained that he stuttered. Pharaoh would laugh at his stammered demands! But God, who didn't need to be told about the stutter, chose Moses anyway. Whether the stutter helped, hurt or went away, Moses succeeded.

And we're like Moses. When God leads us to a bold task, whether large or small, it can make our knees weak. Which is the plan. God is about big things. Things beyond human thought and ability. Things we can't do alone. Things that build confidence for the next adventure.

Sometimes we allow our concerns to harden into concrete and fear stops us. We settle for less than all we were meant to be and do, accepting the good instead of striving for the best.

Or we start, then forget God's help. The task takes longer than we expected. It's hard. Obstacles pop up. Faith wavers, as it always does if we forget the God part of the equation. Substituting willpower for God-power doesn't work.

God's plans require both his assistance and all the talent he "knit" into us, sometimes talent we didn't realize we owned. We accomplish things we wouldn't have thought possible—if we thought of them at all.

# Jesus - An Introduction

---

*B*ut he was wounded for the wrong we did; he was crushed for the evil we did. The punishment, which made us well, was given to him, and we are healed because of his wounds. We all have wandered away like sheep; each of us has gone his own way. But the Lord has put on him the punishment for all the evil we have done.

---

- Isaiah (eye ZAY uh), chapter 53, verses 5 through 6 (Is. 53:5-6)
- New Century Version (NCV)
- The Old Testament prophet, Isaiah, prophesying the life of Jesus Christ. He wrote this approximately 700 years before the birth of Christ. Bible prophets had to be 100 percent accurate or they were considered false prophets. False prophets ended up dead prophets.

# Jesus - An Introduction

The Bible is the history of God's relationship with people. More than just a human history, it shows how God's actions are woven into the fabric of human life. And it reveals humankind's growing understanding of God as this history unfolds.

The Old Testament, the first part of the Bible, introduces God. The second part, the New Testament, continues the story, fulfilling the predictions and promises made in the Old Testament. The New Testament tells of God physically breaking into history with the birth of Jesus, God in human form.

Jesus' mission was twofold. First, being God, he was the ultimate revelation of God. Jesus displayed God's perfection within human limitations. God with skin on, as it were.

Second, he bridged the chasm separating God and people—a chasm caused by sin. Sin's imperfection can't exist alongside a perfect God, and imperfect people cannot fix their imperfection. Jesus is the remedy—the bridge—that solves the problem.

Jesus came to earth as a baby, to experience life as we do. Other than a childhood incident or two, the Bible concentrates on his public ministry, the last three years of his life.

Those three years are well documented. More so than any other life. Thousands of manuscripts document his family, his words and his actions. There's no need to wonder. History gives us more than enough facts, and faith lets us experience the confirmation.

# Trying To Put Jesus In A Box

Dearly loved friends, don't always believe everything you hear just because someone says it is a message from God; test it first to see if it really is. For there are many false teachers around, and the way to find out if the message is from the Holy Spirit is to ask: Does it really agree that Jesus Christ, God's Son, actually became man with a human body? If so, then the message is from God. If not, the message is not from God but from one who is against Christ, like the "Antichrist" you have heard about who is going to come, and his attitude of enmity against Christ is already abroad in the world. Dear young friends, you belong to God and have already won your fight with those who are against Christ because there is someone in your hearts who is stronger than any evil teacher in this wicked world. These men belong to this world so, quite naturally, they are concerned about worldly affairs and the world pays attention to them. But we are children of God; that is why only those who have walked and talked with God will listen to us. Others won't. That is another way to know whether a message is really from God, for if it is, the world won't listen to it.

- John's first letter, chapter 4, verses 1 through 6 (I Jn. 4:1-6)
- The Living Bible (TLB)
- Jesus' disciple talks about how different the mind set of a Christian is from that of a nonbeliever.

# Trying To Put Jesus In A Box

Jesus is God's son. And Jesus is also God. Which fact nobody understands. Theologians have puzzled for years, but this knowledge is beyond human capacity. From beginning to end, though, the Bible says it is so, with facts too tightly woven to dismiss or ignore.

And the fact that Jesus is God puts an end to attempts to overlook his authority and power.

Some say, "Well, Jesus was a good man, but just a man." Others try to put Jesus in a slightly different box, saying, "Jesus was a wonderful teacher and good example, but no more." Still others limit Jesus to the role of prophet.

None of this is new. Jesus heard the same claims and refuted them all. He announced plainly he was God. He is our Savior (English), the Christ (Greek), the Messiah (Hebrew). He left no room for doubt.

But we resist. And here's why: If we can diminish Jesus to mere mortal, we can dismiss the teachings we don't like. Claim they are merely opinions, no better than our own, and selectively decide what we will—or won't—believe. It's a control thing.

But Jesus is God. Since Christianity is based on this fact, we can't be Christians and say otherwise. His words, then, are God's words and not up for dispute.

And when we learn his teaching and understand his heart, we'll wonder why we put up a fight.

# Always a Two-Way Street

*I* can never stop thanking God for all the wonderful gifts he has given you, now that you are Christ's; he has enriched your whole life. He has helped you speak out for him and has given you a full understanding of the truth; what I told you Christ could do for you has happened. Now you have every grace and blessing; every spiritual gift and power for doing his will are yours during this time of waiting for the return of our Lord Jesus Christ.

- Paul's first letter to the Corinthians (kore IN thee unz), chapter 1, verses 4 through 7 (I Cor.1:4-7)

- The Living Bible (TLB)

- Brilliant, successful, born to wealth and privilege, Paul is still amazed at the love God has for him. Corinth is in southern Greece. Starting a church there proved to be a difficult exercise akin to herding cats, but ended up a very worthwhile endeavor. Paul alternates between telling the Corinthians how wonderful they are and ordering them to shape up—kind of like raising children.

# Always A Two-Way Street

Relationships are two-way streets that involve both giving and receiving. If one person in a relationship does all the heavy lifting, it's not a relationship. An obsession perhaps, or maybe a wish, but not a relationship.

Our love relationship with God, then, involves giving and receiving on both sides. God doesn't engage in one-way, make-believe relationships. Bogus commitments benefit no one.

In the relationship, God's part is sure. We know it's his nature is to give, and we ask away.

We're the iffy side of the equation. Are we willing to give God the love and commitment a true relationship requires?

Consider a human example. If you want your beloved to believe your professions of undying devotion, you better back up your words with action. You can't "do your own thing" and leave no time for your beloved; an effort to please and delight has to be part of the plan. Getting to know your beloved better day by day should be a priority. And so on. Without action, words don't mean much.

God requires more than lip service, too. He has to be the center of our lives, the hub that moves everything. Are we willing to spend time reading his words and listening for his voice? To consider whether our actions and choices will benefit the relationship or hurt, even destroy, it?

And here's where the rubber meets the road: If you treat your beloved the way you treat God, will the relationship flourish?

# Who's In Control Here?

*Y*ours, O Lord, are the greatness, the power, the glory, the victory, and the majesty; for all that is in the heavens and on earth is yours; yours is the kingdom, O Lord, and you are exalted as head above all. Riches and honor come from you, and you rule over all. In your hand are power and might; and it is in your hand to make great and to give strength to all. And now, our God, we give thanks to you and praise your glorious name.

- First Chronicles (KRAWHN ih klz), chapter 29, verses 11 through 13 (I Chron. 29:11-13)
- New Revised Standard Version (NRSV)
- The two books of Chronicles tell the history of God's people. Originally, the books were together as one, written, we believe, by the Old Testament prophet, Ezra.

# Who's In Control Here?

What is it about control? People want to control other people, people want to control events, people want to control things as far as the eye can see—and then some.

Give it up! You have no control.

So, let's define. Yes, we should have self-discipline. We should try to do the right thing. We should love the people in our lives. We should provide direction for our children. And we should give our best to whatever we do. We can semi-control ourselves.

But real control? The ability to cause events? Oh, please. We don't know what the next five minutes will bring. Plus, since we don't always know what's best for ourselves, how can we know what's best for anybody else? Human control is a delusion.

Life, though, doesn't just happen. God's in control. He gives us enormous freedom and, looking around, things may appear to be random, but God is firmly in control.

And control can't be divided. We can't give control of our lives both to God and another person because we can't go in two directions. Likewise, we shouldn't attempt to control somebody else. When you get right down to it, attempts to control another person is trying to take God's place.

Christians accept God's control—of our lives, our world, everything. God knows what the future holds, he knows what's best for us, he wants the best for us and, if we cooperate, he can and will make it happen.

Relax.

# ON BEING UNIQUE

The body of Christ [the church] had many different parts, just as any other body does. Our bodies don't have just one part. They have many parts. Suppose a foot says, "I'm not a hand, so I'm not part of the body." Or suppose an ear says, "I'm not an eye, so I'm not part of the body." Wouldn't the ear still belong to the body? If our bodies were only an eye, we couldn't hear a thing. And if they were only an ear, we couldn't smell a thing. But God has put all parts of our body together in the way he decided is best. A body is not really a body, unless there is more than one part. It takes many parts to make a single body. That's why the eyes cannot say they don't need the hands. That's also why the head cannot say it doesn't need the feet. In fact, we cannot get along without the parts of the body that seem to be the weakest.

- First Corinthians (kore IN thee unz), chapter 12, verse 12 and verses 14 through 22 (I Cor. 12:12,14-22)

- The International Student Bible for Catholics—*New Testament Edition* (CEV)

- Paul's first letter to the church he founded in Corinth. Directed at people who thought they were somewhat better than others, this advice is relevant in any age.

## On Being Unique

A lot of parents throw around too many comparisons, usually negative. "Why can't you get good grades like Susie?" "You're clumsier than Joey." "Pam's not as messy as you." "Why can't you be like Charles?"

Comparisons shrivel the soul.

God never compares his children. He knows our name—without rattling through three or four to get to it. He's the very one who created us to be unique. He authored our hopes and dreams. He understands our fears.

Which is not to say we've made it. God accepts us where we are, as we are, but he never leaves us there. We're always in the process of becoming. Becoming what we'll discover when we get there.

God accepts any starting point in our journey with him. What he cares about is that we're on the road with him, faced in the right direction and moving forward as best we can. Others may be further down the road, but God delights in the simple fact we're walking with him.

Sometimes our spiritual journey races along by leaps and bounds. Other times, the going slows to a frustrating plod. And, from time to time, we may wonder if we've stalled out. Don't worry. Enjoy the spiritual growth spurts and be patient through the plateaus, which are usually the best learning times.

It's a life, not a contest. It's your unique journey, planned by God, who knows your name.

# Looking In the Wrong Direction

*S*o what about all these wise men, these scholars, these brilliant debaters of this world's great affairs? God has made them all look foolish and shown their wisdom to be useless nonsense. For God in his wisdom saw to it that the world would never find God through human brilliance, and then he stepped in and saved all those who believed his message, which the world calls foolish and silly.

- Paul's first letter to the church in Corinth, chapter 1, verses 20-21 (I Cor. 1:20-21)
- The Living Bible (TLB)
- Paul writes here based on his own experience. Working diligently to serve God by means of his own impressive brilliance, Paul made himself God's enemy—until God got his attention and turned him around.

# Looking In the Wrong Direction

The church was central to everyday life in Bible times. People spent a lot of time contemplating God.

One prominent church group then was the Pharisees, well-educated men who spent their lives studying scripture and coming up with rules for even trivial details of life. They had status almost equivalent to the rabbis.

One area of intense study was the coming of the Messiah. The Scriptures promised over and over that God would send a Messiah, a Savior, to save his people.

With their nation occupied by the Roman Empire, the Pharisees decided this Messiah would come as a mighty king who would conquer and destroy the hated Romans.

God, however, came as a baby. A helpless baby. Not born to fame or fortune. Born in a stable, with a message of peace. Set on having a mighty king to save them, many Pharisees refused to consider Jesus as their Messiah.

Well, integrating our hopes into what we read so it means what we want it to mean is common. People do it all the time.

But by focusing on their own plans, they missed God's great gift, the long-awaited Savior. Not to mention the follow-on, and even more amazing, gift of God's Spirit to actually come to live in us, to give us power and peace.

Most Pharisees would have none of it. God, they decided, should follow their plans.

How very modern.

*Sometimes you have to do things
you don't want to do to become the person
you always hoped you could be.*

# Maximum Defeat

But God showed his great love for us by sending Christ to die for us while we were still sinners. And since by his blood he did all this for us as sinners, how much more will he do for us now that he has declared us not guilty? Now he will save us from all of God's wrath to come. And since, when we were his enemies, we were brought back to God by the death of his Son, what blessings he must have for us now that we are his friends and he is living within us! Now we rejoice in our wonderful new relationship with God—all because of what our Lord Jesus Christ has done in dying for our sins—making us friends of God.

- Romans, chapter 5, verses 8 through 11 (Rom. 5:8-11)
- The Living Bible (TLB)
- Paul's letter to the church in Rome. This is Paul's longest letter, written to expound his understanding of God to the large and thriving church at Rome. The people there knew Paul only by reputation, and this letter prepared them for his planned visit. When Paul finally made it to Rome, he arrived as a prisoner on his way to martyrdom.

# Maximum Defeat

As defeats go, being nailed to a tree, suffering and suffocating—after long hours of torturous pain when you no longer had strength to breathe—would seem to top the list. This death, crucifixion, is the cruelest possible way to kill somebody. So cruel, in fact, that Rome, who invented it, would not allow Roman citizens to suffer it. Rome intended it as a lesson to anybody foolish enough to challenge its authority.

Crucifixion was always very public. Crowds gathered to picnic, jeering as they watched people beg and plead for their lives. As a mission of mercy, ladies from the church came to offer painkilling drugs to those being crucified.

Everybody feared crucifixion. And yet Jesus died shouting victory. People who had gathered to mock went home dismayed at their spoiled fun. Roman soldiers, whose daily job was crucifying one person after another, stood in awe, shocked to realize Jesus really was God.

A completely innocent man. The only perfect human ever. Crucified for what? Willing to suffer unimaginable pain without complaint. Why?

Because it accomplished the main reason he came: To pay the price required by our sin. And he did it willingly, even for those who want nothing to do with him.

This is love, love written in red. For you. For me.

# GRAVE CLOTHES

When it was evening, there came a rich man from Arimathea (air ih muh THEE ah), named Joseph, who was also a disciple of Jesus. He went to [Governor] Pilate and asked for the body of Jesus; then Pilate ordered it to be given to him. So Joseph took the body and wrapped it in a clean linen cloth and laid it in his own new tomb, which he had hewn in the rock. He then rolled a great stone to the door of the tomb and went away.

- The gospel written by Matthew, chapter 27, verses 57 through 60 (Matt. 27:57-60)
- New Revised Standard Version (NRSV)
- The story of Jesus' burial as told by his disciple, Matthew. Joseph of Arimathea risked everything—including his life—with his action. The enormous cost of a hand-chiseled tomb, along with Joseph's high status as a person who could go directly to Pilate and ask for a favor, gives us an indication of his great wealth. Regular people used caves as tombs.

# GRAVE CLOTHES

To fully understand reports of Jesus' resurrection, we need to know how bodies were prepared for burial in those days. Especially the part about the so-called grave clothes.

Two things were needed to prepare a body for burial: Spices plus yards and yards of linen cloth about eleven inches wide.

A Pharisee named Nicodemus provided the spices, myrrh and a little aloe, for Jesus' burial. In fact, he provided about 100 pounds of spices—enough for a royal burial. Jesus was not buried as a pauper. His grave clothes would last for centuries.

The spices were ground into a paste and brushed on the cloth as it was wrapped around the body. Wrapping started at the feet and, with the arms raised, overlapped layer upon layer up to the chest. Then the arms were lowered, and the brushing and wrapping restarted at the fingertips, stopping at the neck.

A small piece of cloth was knotted in the corners and put on the head.

The wrapped body was laid on one end of a long piece of cloth. The other end of the cloth was brought over the head and body as a covering.

When the spices dried in a day or so, the grave clothes became like concrete. A concrete cocoon around the body.

When Jesus came out of the grave, those grave clothes—that cocoon—were empty, but undisturbed.

This is, of course, not humanly possible. It's no wonder people were perplexed about the meaning of it all. Some people still are.

# Dead, Absolutely Dead

The next day, the one after Preparation Day, the chief priests and the Pharisees went to [Governor] Pilate. "Sir," they said, "we remember that while he was still alive that deceiver [referring to Jesus] said, 'After three days I will rise again.' So give the order for the tomb to be made secure until the third day. Otherwise, his disciples may come and steal the body and tell the people that he has been raised from the dead. This last deception will be worse than the first." "Take a guard" Pilate answered. "Go, make the tomb as secure as you know how." So they [Roman soldiers] went and made the tomb secure by putting a seal on the stone and posting the guard.

- Disciple Matthew's gospel, chapter 27, verses 62 through 66 (Matt. 27:62-66)
- New International Version (NIV)
- Written to Jewish Christians, this passage describes the extreme lengths the church leaders went to make sure Jesus could not make good on his promise to come back to life the third day after his death.

# Dead, Absolutely Dead

The Roman Empire was purposefully vicious. Brutality kept conquered nations in fear; challenging Rome meant risking a horrible death. And within the Roman military system, anybody who failed an assigned task paid, as painfully as possible, with his life.

Jesus' crucifixion was handled by a team of four Roman soldiers whose job, day in and day out, was to crucify people. One soldier's duty was to know the "sweet spot" for driving in the spikes so bodies didn't fall off crosses. Another soldier certified death. Failure by one soldier meant the death of all four. And their expert opinion was that Jesus was absolutely dead.

But, because Jesus had promised to come back to life in three days, precautions were taken to make sure he stayed dead. The Roman seal was put on the two-ton boulder that covered the entrance to Jesus' tomb. Anybody tampering with this seal was crucified upside-down, the ultimate in suffering.

In case the seal wasn't sufficiently intimidating, a *custodia*—which could be either twelve or sixteen Roman soldiers—guarded the tomb entrance, each heavily armed and expected to fully defend an area of six square feet. In case of failure, the *custodia* was tied together and set ablaze.

So it was set. The soldiers and the seal would guard the tomb for the three critical days, well past the time Jesus' grave clothes became rock hard. Escape was impossible. The problem would be over.

They thought they had everything under control.

But God had other plans.

# ONE SUNDAY MORNING

*M*ary Magdalene went and said to the followers, "I saw the Lord!" And she told them what Jesus had said to her.

- The gospel written by John, chapter 20, verse 18 (John 20:18)
- New Century Version (NCV)
- John's recounting of Easter (resurrection) morning. After Mary Magdalene came with this news, the disciples John and Peter ran to see what had happened at the tomb, thus becoming two of the more than 500 eyewitnesses to the fact that Jesus returned to life on the third day after his death—as he said he would.

# ONE SUNDAY MORNING

It was over. Jesus was dead. His terrified disciples scattered, hiding behind closed doors lest the Romans kill them, too. Hope died along with Jesus.

As the sun rose Sunday morning, women came to the tomb, bringing more burial spices to put on Jesus' body, the traditional practice. As they walked, they discussed who would move the huge stone covering the tomb's entrance. They didn't know about the additional complications of the Roman seal and guards added after they left the tomb Friday afternoon.

Arriving at the tomb, they saw the stone already rolled away, far away and up a small incline. The guards, knowing the penalty for failure, had gone to seek protection. The tomb was open and abandoned. Looking in, they saw the grave clothes. But Jesus was gone.

They thought something terrible had happened—again. As they sat crying, Jesus came and gently spoke to them. He sent them to tell the disciples he was alive, that he had conquered death as he said he would.

Jesus was alive!

And so began the resurrection of hope. Hope, now knowledge, that continues. Jesus is God, he is alive and he offers his life to us.

Christians celebrate the resurrection each week by gathering together on Sunday, the Lord's Day, to worship. On Sundays, we need to celebrate.

Jesus is alive. He is with us. Indeed, he is in us.

# A Credible Witness

*For* I am the least worthy of all the apostles, and I shouldn't even be called an apostle at all after the way I treated the church of God. But whatever I am now it is all because God poured out such kindness and grace upon me—and not without results: for I have worked harder than all the other apostles, yet actually I wasn't doing it, but God working in me, to bless me.

- Paul's first letter to the Corinthians (kore IN thee unz), chapter 15, verses 9 through 10 (I Cor.15:9-10)

- The Living Bible (TLB)

- Paul never forgot where he started or how far God brought him. Speaking over the years, his almost rhapsodic words still reveal his amazement and joy.

# A Credible Witness

After he came back to life, hundreds of people saw Jesus at various times, in various places, doing various things. The Bible and histories of the day record these events. Even so, not everybody believes the resurrection actually happened.

But consider Paul. At the time of Jesus' death, Paul hated Jesus and everything he said and did. Well-educated, a fast-rising young star in the church, Paul believed Jesus was dangerous, a charismatic charlatan. Paul spent his days trying to destroy this new movement. His vendetta included putting Jesus' followers in jail, with a recommendation of death.

Part of his anger arose from the fact nobody could find Jesus' body. Everybody knew the tomb's location. And they tracked the movements of Jesus' followers. But nobody could find the body.

Further, the disciples insisted they saw Jesus alive and well, that he talked and ate with them. If Paul could produce Jesus' body, the disciple's story would fall apart, and Jesus would be just another failed prophet.

That was Paul's goal.

Then Paul encountered the resurrected Jesus, and his life made one huge U-turn.

Paul became an ardent follower of the same Jesus he had persecuted. His exploits are described in the Bible, in the book called *Acts*. His letters, now a significant part of the Bible, proclaim and explain the fact Jesus is God's true and only son. And Paul died for his new faith.

Given Paul's original hatred of Jesus, his amazing turnaround makes him a completely credible witness.

# Why?

*T*his is how God showed his love to us: He sent his one and only Son into the world so that we could have life through him. This is what real love is: It is not our love for God; it is God's love for us in sending his Son to be the way to take away our sins.

- Disciple John's first letter, chapter 4, verses 9 through 10 (I Jn. 4:9-10)
- New Century Version (NCV)
- If you are new to the Bible, this letter and John's gospel are good places to start.

# Why?

The question haunts history: Why did Jesus have to be crucified for our sin? Did it have to be so cruel and ugly?

Couldn't God just say, "Abracadabra" or boom out some heavenly command? Something less overwhelming than a gory crucifixion?

No. Had there been another way, God would have taken it.

Our sin-riddled imperfection creates a barrier to a relationship with God, the very thing we need to obtain inner peace. Only a perfect, sinless sacrifice, which we can't provide, could make such a prize possible. God, loving us even in our helplessness, gave his son as the needed sacrifice.

Sin always costs a lot, but we rarely see it that way. We grade sin. Some sins are biggies, we say, but most we excuse. God, though, doesn't grade on a curve; sin is sin. Period. We may trivialize sin and decide it's not a big deal, but God knows it's a huge deal. It cost him his son.

In addition to the price he paid, God hates sin because of what it does to us. Sin drags us down like an anchor. It clouds our joy and destroys our peace. Sin builds walls that block us from God's best for us.

Away from God, we can't see this. But as God's love embraces us and God's Spirit guides us, we begin to understand. Awe staggers us when we realize God sees us as valuable, well worth the price he paid.

And then we know: We are the why.

# CASTLES IN THE AIR

*T*he poor, deluded fool feeds on ashes. He is trusting something that can give him no help at all. Yet he cannot bring himself to ask "Is this thing, this idol that I'm holding in my hand, a lie?"

- Isaiah (eye ZAY uh), chapter 44, verse 20 (Is. 44:20)
- New Living Translation (NLT)
- Written by the Old Testament prophet, Isaiah, in about 700 B.C. Isaiah is considered to be the greatest of the writing prophets and was perhaps the most prominent prophet in the Old Testament (the first part of the Bible).

# Castles In the Air

Everybody promotes self-esteem. Self-esteem adds color to life. Without it, life isn't satisfying.

Okay. So how do we get this wonderful thing?

The answer used to be about setting lofty goals and working hard to reach them. Self-esteem was earned. Be kind. Be ethical. Our achievements built the foundation of self-esteem.

But some worried about having requirements. Goals might narrow our vision. Lofty goals could bring disappointment, perhaps even failure. Striving toward goals took time away from smelling roses.

Self-esteem, they asserted, should come simply from being. No goals. No standards. No plans. Whatever we are is wonderful. Celebrate whatever that is. People are inherently good. Every day we're all getting better and better. Affirm it, and it will be.

Self-esteem, then, is built on thin air. I'm ok; you're ok.

Which gives us the spectacle of juvenile delinquents celebrating their self-esteem by bashing people as a charming exercise in self-expression.

But, even for the honest, loyal, brave and true, is coasting through life enough? Without effort to achieve something? Without goals?

This doesn't work. Without some kind of focus we're empty, living lives of day following day in varying shades of gray. And we face our so-called golden years with regrets and if-onlys.

Self-esteem castles constructed on thin air demean us and belittle our dreams.

We're worth more than that.

*Life is lumpy.*

# Comparative Confidence

*G*od saved you by his special favor when you believed. And you can't take credit for this; it is a gift from God. Salvation is not a reward for the good things we have done, so none of us can boast about it. For we are God's masterpiece. He has created us anew in Christ Jesus, so that we can do the good things he planned for us long ago.

- Ephesians (ee FEE zhunz), chapter 2, verses 8 through 10
- New Living Translation (NLT)
- Paul's letter to the church he founded in Ephesus (F uh suss). This letter was written to encourage those in the faith, many of whom came from paganism or the worship of cosmic forces.

# Comparative Confidence

Since castles in the sky have a habit of falling down and self-esteem "just because" doesn't work, what do we do?

We're back to earning self-esteem.

And lofty goals and hard work do turn out to please the soul. We climb the ladder of success. We create a happy home. We hit a home run—as our kids watch. It straightens the shoulders to be able to stand back and say, "I did that," whatever "that" is.

And if, somewhere between start and finish, failure looks like a real possibility, finishing well is doubly satisfying. Lofty goals make us sweat, but they bring big rewards.

Intangible goals can add bounce to our steps, too. Perhaps telling the truth when a lie or silence would be easier. Doing the right thing instead of the popular thing. They can please our souls even when nobody knows.

But sometimes we don't reach our goals. Or we see success that exceeds our own. Our happy home disintegrates into squabbles. Perhaps truth slips away from time to time. Or we watch the ground wash out from under our feet for reasons outside ourselves. Life's like that.

We need a foundation beyond achievement. A foundation that doesn't depend on comparisons to others, one that doesn't end in disappointment or wash away. One that fills our need for meaning. Where do we go for that?

# A GOOD FOUNDATION IS A SOLID FOUNDATION

O Lord, our Lord, your greatness is seen in all the world!
Your praise reaches up to the heavens;
It is sung by children and babies.
You are safe and secure from all your enemies;
You stop anyone who opposes you.
When I look at the sky, which you have made,
At the moon and the stars, which you set in their places—
What is man [mankind], that you think of him;
Mere man, that you care for him?
Yet you made him inferior only to yourself,
You crowned him with glory and honor.
You appointed him ruler over everything you made;
You placed him over all creation;
Sheep and cattle, and wild animals too;
The birds and the fish and the creatures in the seas.
O Lord, our Lord, your greatness is seen in all the world!

- Psalm (silent P, rhymes with palm) 8 (Ps. 8)

- Today's English Version (TEV)

- A poem of worship and praise written by ancient Israel's King David

# A Good Foundation Is a Solid Foundation

If thin air and achievement fail, where can we find a self-esteem foundation that doesn't disappoint or disappear? In a relationship with God—and nowhere else.

God is the solid, guaranteed-forever, all time big kahuna self-esteem foundation.

Think about it. The Bible says God "knit you together in your mother's womb." Genetics can't begin to tell the full story of you. You were God's idea in the first place.

God put in you the talent, intelligence and personality you need to achieve his plans for your life. His plans for your role in what happens in our universe.

You're not an extra in a cast of thousands to God. He created you to be unique; he delights in you. You are like no other.

Besides creating your custom-made self, God, in his eternal wisdom, declares you important. He knows your name, your hopes, your dreams, your fears, your secrets. Even how many hairs are on your head.

And, finally, he gave his only Son to pay the price of providing you a way to come home. And he did it willingly, knowing it would break his heart.

What more is there to say? God, creator of all that is or ever will be, knows you by name, he values you and he loves you. All you have to do is love him back.

Now there's a self-esteem foundation that works.

# Don't Believe Everything You Hear About God

*For the truth about God is known to them instinctively. God has put this knowledge in their hearts. From the time the world was created, people have seen the earth and sky and all that God made. They can clearly see his invisible qualities—his eternal power and divine nature. So they have no excuse whatsoever for not knowing God.*

- Romans, chapter 1, verses 19 through 21 (Rom. 1:19-21)
- New Living Translation (NLT)
- Paul's letter to the church in Rome explaining God's message was realized in Jesus Christ's life and teaching. Both brilliant and practical, Paul didn't mince words.

# Don't Believe Everything You Hear About God

There are, perhaps, a bazillion rumors about God floating around. How God sees us, what God expects of us, what ticks him off and so on. All kinds of rumors, from every direction.

One rumor insists we should live in constant guilt, but God doesn't think so. Now, sometimes guilt is good because it steers us from wrong. If we feel guilt, we repent, ask God for forgiveness and we're done with it. Immediate repentance equals immediate relief. No long days and nights of fretting guilt are required.

Another rumor says since God loves us, he rewards any kind of behavior. Please. God paid an enormous price for us to live large in a loving relationship with him. If we love God, we can't purposely live a life that breaks his heart and still expect him to think it's swell. If we don't love God, then we refuse his love and choose not to have a relationship; he can't reward that. God's full of rewards, but not for bad behavior.

Then there's the rumor that says God takes no part in our lives. That he's "out there, somewhere, watching," which makes God sound more like a stalker than a friend.

We're inundated with misinformation about God. How can we know what's true?

Here's how: We get to know him. As we learn what the Bible says, pray and walk out our faith, God reveals the truth about himself.

Knowing somebody immunizes you from phony-baloney rumors.

# Don't Travel Alone

When I think of the wisdom and scope of his plan, I fall down on my knees and pray to the Father of all the great family of God—some of them already in heaven and some down here on earth—that out of his glorious, unlimited resources he will give you the mighty inner strengthening of his Holy Spirit. And I pray that Christ will be more and more at home in your hearts, living within you as you trust him. May your roots go down deep into the soil of God's marvelous love; and may you be able to feel and understand, as all God's children should, how long, how wise, how deep, and how high his love really is; and to experience this love for yourselves, though it is so great that you will never see the end of it or fully know or understand it. And so at last you will be filled up with God himself.

- Ephesians (ee FEE zhunz), chapter 3, verses 14 through 19 (Eph. 3:14-19)

- The Living Bible (TLB)

- Paul's letter to the church he founded in Ephesus (F uh suss). He was imprisoned in Rome, awaiting death, when he wrote this letter.

# Don't Travel Alone

The Christian life isn't a solitary journey. Christians, Jesus insisted, need to be part of a community of believers. Usually this means finding a church.

It may not be the church in which you grew up. It may not be the most convenient church. It may not be a lot of things, but one thing it must be. It must be a welcoming, spiritually encouraging community.

You'll have to hunt, but there is a community of believers for you. You'll choose from a smorgasbord of possibilities. Some differences are inconsequential. Formal or informal services. Contemporary or traditional music. Large or small. These are cosmetic, not essential, differences.

But some things are crucial. A church should reflect Christ's love—welcoming, accepting and encouraging. Your soul should feel fed and nourished.

And people are important. The people in the church, especially smaller groups within it, will be your teachers, cheerleaders, support group, the people who help keep you on track—your church family.

Now, people aren't perfect. While they may be "going on to perfection," as one church has it, they're not there yet. But when you find people who make God a priority, you've found gold.

Most likely, they'll be in a church that has power, where the preacher has more than a theoretical acquaintance with God and where people are hungry to know more about God. Hungry people go where the food is. And they look for a banquet, not carrot sticks.

Join that happy, hungry crowd. Don't travel alone.

# GOD IS NOT RUNNING FOR SHERIFF

*D*o not be deceived; God cannot be mocked. A man reaps what he sows. The one who sows to please his sinful nature, from that nature will reap destruction; the one who sows to please the Spirit, from the Spirit will reap eternal life.

- Galations (guh LAY shunz), chapter 6, verses 7 through 8 (Gal. 6:7–8)
- New International Version (NIV)
- Paul's letter to the churches he founded in Galatia (guh LAY sha). Throughout the Bible, God tells us we are responsible for our words and actions, which Paul affirms here. Galatia was a large province of many cities.

# GOD IS NOT RUNNING FOR SHERIFF

Where do people get the idea God is up for election? That God will have to give up his job if we vote against him? They say, "Well, I don't believe in God." and seem to think that removes God from office. And takes away the perks of his office, such as the authority to define right and wrong.

Well, no. God is God. He's not running for sheriff. He's not running for president. He's not even running for Pope.

We don't have a vote about whether God gets to be God. Our only choice is whether or not we want God to lead our lives. It's our choice. He won't kidnap us and demand our love. Love is always voluntary.

But, while God doesn't run for office, he campaigns vigorously. Day and night. He gives us the Bible as his campaign literature. He puts campaign volunteers in our path at the most coincidental times. He even sends his Spirit to woo us.

It's a strange campaign. God doesn't campaign for himself, but for us. He makes a huge effort—all to take away our spiritual blindness so we can see how much he loves us and to gain the opportunity to give us a prize we don't deserve and can't possibly earn.

Voting is optional, but not voting means "no." And God keeps his job, whatever we do.

God campaigns, but the win or the loss is ours.

# EVERYBODY BELIEVES IN SOMETHING

*In the past you did not know God. You were slaves to gods that were not real. But now you know the true God.*

- Galatians (guh LAY shunz), chapter 4, verse 8 (Gal. 4:8)
- New Century Version (NCV)
- Paul's letter to the churches in Galatia (guh LAY sha). Church leaders, who worked themselves into positions of leadership after Paul left Galatia, were misleading the people into a do-it-yourself religion instead of a relationship with God. Paul tells the Galatians they're nuts, but two thousand years later, we're still fiddling with some of the same stuff.

# Everybody Believes In Something

Believing is as much a part of us as breathing. We want to believe. We need to believe. And we will believe. In something.

As children, we believed life was fair. That honesty and hard work were always rewarded. That rewards were always earned. But real life got in the way, and we learned to question that belief.

We want to believe in the people in our lives—family, teachers, friends, co-workers, whomever. Many people play many roles to make up the fabric of our lives, and we want them to be worthy of our trust. Fortunately, many are.

But we find out that many people are good about staying around while the sun shines, but disappear when clouds gather. Sometimes even a cloud as small as discomfort with not knowing what to say. Life's storms destroy relationships that seemed to be solid. When storms rage, who stays and who goes is almost always a surprise. People can let us down, sometimes without intending to.

We also believe in things—money, power, success. Over time, each one lets us down. Things are less reliable than people.

The only sure thing is God. He doesn't fail, and he doesn't leave us. His dependability reassures us more each year. We revel in his constant love. We're never alone.

That's not to say life is always easy. Or that learning to rely on God is automatic or instinctual. Life and faith both take work.

But since we're going to believe, we might as well believe in a winner.

# Throw Away the Scale

*G*od made peace through the blood of Christ's death on the cross. At one time you were separated from God. You were his enemies in your minds, and the evil things you did were against God. But now God has made you his friends again. He did this through Christ's death in the body so that he might bring you into God's presence as people who are holy, with no wrong, and with nothing of which can judge you guilty.

- Colossians (cuh LAH shunz), chapter 1, verses 19 through 22 (Col. 1:19-22)

- New Century Version (NCV)

- Paul's letter to the church in Colossae (cuh LAH sigh). Paul was distressed that dishonest leaders were leading the people into worshiping angels and other mystical practices. Paul writes that it is Christ—and Christ alone—who makes us righteous.

# Throw Away the Scale

Some people see God as the great scale-keeper in the sky. He holds, they believe, a scale of justice. Our good deeds are placed on one side, our bad deeds on the other. Upon our arrival at "the pearly gates," the scale will swing up and down finding its balance. If the good deeds outweigh the bad, the doors to heaven open. If the bad deeds are heavier, we descend into hell.

In a word, no. Even our best efforts won't earn residency in heaven. And bad deeds can be forgiven; they don't have to doom us.

What does make the difference in our final destination? We have to accept Jesus' death as payment for our sins. When we make Jesus our boss—our Lord—God counts his perfection as ours. With that, heaven is guaranteed.

Many people don't see it this way. Some believe they're good enough on their own without God, admirable even, and certainly better than others. Others, if they think of God at all, think it ludicrous to put their excellent plans at the disposal of a God they can't see.

But the Bible's clear: Heaven's doors open only to people whom God counts as perfect, which, without a doubt, takes Jesus' intervention.

But this doesn't make sense to those satisfied with their own self-sufficiency. Fully persuaded they're good enough, they live and die by a scale that isn't there.

*Being who you really are
in front of the whole world takes courage,
but a lot less effort than pretending
to be something you're not.*

# Who Is Your Audience?

*O*bviously, I'm not trying to be a people pleaser! No, I am trying to please God. If I were still trying to please people, I would not be Christ's servant.

- Galatians (guh LAY shunz), chapter 1, verse 10 (Gal. 1:10)
- New Living Translation (NLT)
- Paul's letter to the churches in Galatia. Paul wrote all his letters during his times in prison for his faith. This letter reveals his frustration with the people willing to believe lies when they already know truth.

# Who Is Your Audience?

Who is your audience? Whom do you try to please with your life? To impress as you sing the songs of your heart and do the dance called life?

For most, the audience is everybody else. We want to look "in." Wear the right clothes. Drive the right car. Live in the right neighborhood. Even use the right vocabulary.

Okay, everybody stand in a circle. Now impress the person on your right. Next, impress the person on your left. Talk about empty calories.

If we're always breaking our necks—and bank accounts—to be like everybody else, how do we discover who we are? Do we sing, "I gotta be me, whoever that is?"

Some use parents as their audience, especially parents who never applauded them. They strive and strive, even as adults, to find the magic key that will make them realize they're worth loving.

But there's no magic key because the problem was never about lovability. Rejection is rarely about the rejected; it's about the audience.

A good audience is made up of coaches and encouragers.

Of course, God is the perfect audience, but we need a human audience, too. Look for people who share your goals and, like God, delight in you, help you through rough patches and always choose you for their team.

People who, also like God, hear the song in your heart even when you're unable to sing it. Then do the same for them.

# STATUS AND POWER

*I* do not cease to give thanks for you as I remember you in my prayers. I pray that the God of our Lord Jesus Christ, the Father of glory, may give you a spirit of wisdom and revelation as you come to know him, so that, with the eyes of your heart enlightened, you may know what is the hope to which he has called you, what are the riches of his glorious inheritance among the saints [believers], and what is the immeasurable greatness of his power for us who believe, according to the working of his great power.

- Ephesians (ee FEE zhunz), chapter 1, verses 16 through 19 (Eph. 1:16-19)
- New Revised Standard Version (NRSV)
- Paul's letter to the flourishing church he founded in Ephesus (F uh suss) where his colleagues Priscilla and Aquila lived and worked.

# Status and Power

Wealth brings status. Fame does, too. Position works, as well. Maybe not a lot of status and perhaps not forever, but we pirouette the status dance for the power it gives to a chosen few.

But when wealth meets wealthier, status sinks. The mayor meets the Queen, and status resides with the Queen. And so it goes.

Then God changes the rules by inviting everybody to get power from a relationship with him, regardless of wealth, fame or position. Better yet, this relationship plants our feet on solid ground, so when other sources of status slip away, we'll still be standing.

Sounds good. We accept, but not always to universal huzzahs.

Friends and family may prefer us to chase non-God power. Our new life may discombobulate their comfort level. While their idea of life, status or power can't match what we have, temptation can sing its enticing melodies loudly.

That's when we need to remember that our focus inevitably becomes our god. If we focus on money, whether we have any or not, money's our god. Same with fame or position. Our heart and our treasure are always in the same place.

There's never enough of whatever's tempting us to make it worth losing God. Without God, we lack his power to reach the dreams he authored in our hearts. What's worth losing that?

Not that there's anything wrong with money, position and fame in their place. They just make lousy gods.

# ABOUT THIS FORGIVING THING

*If another believer sins, rebuke him; then if he repents, forgive him. Even if he wrongs you seven times a day and each time turns again and asks forgiveness, forgive him.*

- The gospel written by Luke, chapter 17, verses 3 and 4 (Luke 17:3-4)
- New Living Translation (NLT)
- The words of Jesus, teaching his disciples. Luke, who worked with Paul, also wrote the book of Acts which recounts the days of the early church.

*He [Jesus] never sinned, and he never deceived anyone. He did not retaliate when he was insulted. When he suffered, he did not threaten to get even. He left his case in the hands of God, who always judges fairly.*

- First Peter, chapter 2, verses 22 and 23 (I Pet. 2:22-23)
- New Living Translation (NLT)
- Peter's first letter to the church at large. Peter was the leader of Jesus' closest group of twelve disciples and, along with Paul, the leader of the new church.

# ABOUT THIS FORGIVING THING

When we get hurt, we're told to "forgive and forget." No matter who, no matter what, forgive and forget. Sounds noble, even righteous. Take the high road. Don't be judgmental.

Wrong.

First, forgetting is silly. Living and learning are based on remembering.

Forgiving is the struggle. Let's look at God's example.

Whenever sinners repent, God forgives, willingly and gladly. But God never forgives unrepented sin. He paid far too high a price to be casual about sin.

God's standard is our standard. We forgive repented sins against us fully and freely, but we don't reward unrepented sin by forgiving it. We can't hand out forgiveness willy-nilly. As we're accountable for our actions, we have to allow others to be accountable for theirs.

But what do we do when those who wound us never accept responsibility for their actions, never ask our forgiveness? Holding onto hurt destroys us. Making pain a trophy kills life. Seeking revenge eats us alive. What do we do with our anger, our pain, our confusion?

We give it to God and let it go. He knows the hearts of those who hurt us, so he knows whether to forgive them or not.

Then we let God heal our pain and give us wisdom to deal with the consequences of what happened. We trust God to bring good from it.

We move on from our suffering and let the hurters work it out with God, who is not amused that they wounded his child.

# DESIGNER GODS

*D*on't let anyone lead you astray with empty philosophy and high-sounding nonsense that come from human thinking and from the evil powers of this world, and not from Christ. For in Christ the fullness of God lives in a human body, and you are complete through your union with Christ.

- Colossians (cuh LAH shunz), chapter 2, verses 8 through 10 (Col. 2:8-10)
- New Living Translation (NLT)
- Paul's letter to the church at Colossae (cuh LAH sigh). Paul had never been to this church, but his heart was intensely involved with the believers there.

# DESIGNER GODS

Gods designed to sanction a chosen point of view are always in style. They tend to be built on-the-fly, with, as might be expected, uncertain results.

Some design a situational god. They make decisions to bless current circumstances, adding a hope here, a thought there, to construct a god who dependably affirms their decisions, however self-defeating. After many turns in the road, their god is a jumble of half-remembered desires, signifying not much of anything. They don't know why they're unhappy.

Others prefer a Mary Poppins god, one they can count on to pat them on the head and say "Good job." Decisions are unnecessary, growing up a bore. All that's needed is a spoonful of sugar to help the medicine, which cures anything, go down. They don't know why they're unhappy.

Of course, "me" makes a popular god. Deep inside, some say, is the god who is you. The true, spiritual you. Not above you, not beyond you, but you. The focus is always self. Unfortunately, gods no larger or more powerful than ourselves leave willpower as our only weapon combat life's difficulties. And they wonder—well, you know.

Designer gods are comfortable. They make no demands. They require no effort.

But when life's storms come roaring in, these gods of our invention offer no peace, no power beyond our own frail frames and no wisdom to guide us. We're alone, pummeled by the fury of the storm.

# SHIFTING SANDS

*S*o then, anyone who hears these words of mine and obeys them is like a wise man who built his house on rock. The rain poured down, the rivers flooded over, and the wind blew hard against that house. But it did not fall, because it was built on rock. But anyone who hears these words of mine and does not obey them is like a foolish man who built his house on sand. The rain poured down, the rivers flooded over, the wind blew hard against that house, and it fell. And what a terrible fall that was.

- The gospel written by Matthew, chapter 7, verses 24 through 27 (Matt. 7:24-27)
- Today's English Version (TEV)
- The words of Jesus about the fact we each build a house, which we call a life, and how well we build determines how well we live.

# SHIFTING SANDS

Desert rains are sudden and fierce. Desert roads have dips called "washes" where run off from the squall-like storms rushes through.

Washes are treacherous. The water is always deeper than it appears. Few realize the power of angry, rushing water until it's too late.

Adding to the danger is sandy desert soil that rushes along with the water. But out of sight, well below the water's surface.

Driving through a running wash can mean attempting to drive on shifting sand, without contact with the road, without traction. At which point, the force of the water can wash a car away, tumbling it down the wash like a toy.

Life has storms, too. Jesus told a story about two men, two houses and a storm.

The first man built well. He dug down to bedrock to make the foundation solid. Then he built a solid house on that solid foundation. When the storm came, the house stood.

The second man built easy. Since it is easier to dig sand than pickax your way through rock, he quickly—and cleverly, he thought—built his house on sand. When the storm came, the house fell.

Every day we build the life we live in. How well we build determines how well it stands. God offers us a solid rock foundation. Then, as we move through life, God keeps us in contact with the road and provides the traction we need to stay on course.

Anything else is shifting sand.

# You Can Count On Consequences

*So when you are offering your gift at the altar, if you remember that your brother or sister [another believer] has something against you, leave your gift there before the altar and go first to be reconciled to your brother or sister, and then come and offer your gift.*

- The gospel written by Matthew, chapter 5, verses 23 through 24 (Matt. 5:23-24)
- New Revised Standard Version (NRSV)
- The words of Jesus telling us not to act all holy in church if we hurt or take advantage of people outside of church.

# You Can Count On Consequences

Actions have consequences. Words do, too.

We don't like consequences. In fact, we want to be excused from any consequences. We want a Teflon coating.

Of course, consequences can be good. Do life right, and the results are good. Which we like.

The problem is negative consequences. We hurt somebody. Our word turns out not to be our bond. We remain silent while people are destroyed by gossip. And now we have to make it right. It's hard, and we don't want to do it.

We don't want to own up to what we did. To admit we were a whole lot less than wonderful. Less than we know we could be. And certainly less than we know we should be.

Some think there's an easy way out. They reason if they pray and ask God's forgiveness, that will end the matter right there. Slick, quick and, best of all, no need to go public.

Well, God does forgive. But forgiveness doesn't erase consequences. If we've hurt anybody, we need to make it right. Ease the pain we caused. Make good on our commitments.

Being God's child isn't simply a matter of fine words. It's about being a force for good.

Fortunately, we're not in this alone. God goes with us, bracing us with grace and courage to do what has to be done.

And as we go, he accepts our sincere efforts—whether anybody else does or not.

# MOVING ON UP

Happy are those who don't listen to the wicked,
who don't go where sinners go,
who don't do what evil people do.
They love the Lord's teachings, and they think about
    those teachings day and night.
They are strong, like a tree planted by a river.
That produces fruit in season
and its leaves don't die
Everything they do will succeed.
But wicked people are not like that.
They are like chaff that the wind blows away.
So the wicked will not escape God's punishment.
Sinners will not worship with God's people.
This is because the Lord takes care of his people,
but the wicked will be destroyed.

- The Psalms (silent P, rhymes with palms), chapter 1 (Ps. 1)

- New Century Version (NCV)

- Psalms are poems—prayers—that were set to music as hymns. The Psalms include every possible emotion. You will especially appreciate Psalms when life is in turmoil.

# Moving On Up

"Birds of a feather flock together" is an old, but still relevant, saying about how we seek to link up with people who look like us. Our group.

To stay in the group, we behave like others in the group. We do things we might not do alone. Agitators know if one person in some mob throws rocks, the others will follow.

Mob psychology works in reverse, also. Actions toward doing something wrong can be stopped if one person says "no," allowing the others to fit in on either side. If nobody speaks up, though, the actions continue.

Knowing this, rather than the usual default of trying to fit in with the most available group, we need to find a group that fits us. If we want encouragement in striving toward our goals, we need people with similar goals, people whose intentions for God match ours.

It's easy to talk about changing the company we keep, especially when we bandy about proclamations of growth. But actual change, although a natural part of a growing life, is difficult.

And change begets more change. As we walk with God, we become more like God. Our interests change. Our values deepen. We are, after all, new creations.

We begin to have less in common with those unwilling to grow with us or to share our new life. Mutual interests fade away. We don't fit anymore. We need to move on.

The good news is that more than just moving on, we're moving on up!

*God works to get our attention*
*so he can let us know*
*how wonderful he thinks we are—*
*and how much more he knows we can be.*

# Parlor Tricks

*A*nd the devil said unto him [Jesus], If thou be the Son of God, command this stone that it be made bread. And Jesus answered him, saying, It is written, That man shall not live by bread alone, but by every word of God.

- The Gospel of Luke, Chapter 4, Verses 3 through 4 (Luke 4:3-4)

- King James Version (KJV)

- One of three recorded temptations in which Satan tried to tempt Jesus into doing something spectacular just for show. Jesus simply quotes Scripture to him, and ignores the suggestion to do a "trick."

# Parlor Tricks

In olden days, the parlor was a special room used only for guests. Nowadays we'd compare it to our living rooms, but nobody ever entered the parlor except to clean or entertain guests.

And entertain it was. Family members learned "parlor tricks" to amaze and delight their guests. Usually they were card tricks or magic tricks.

The trick—then as now—was to fool the beholder's eyes. While performing a feat, the trickster attempted to divert the guests' attention with clever talk, jokes and unnecessary gestures.

The only point of parlor tricks was to amuse and entertain. Along with polite conversation, it made a pleasant way to spend an afternoon.

Many people think God's in the parlor trick business. He ought, for their amusement and amazement, to do miracles on demand. Perhaps materialize a change in circumstances to regale—and benefit—them. Not because they want a relationship with God, but because they'd like to use God as their celestial "gofer."

God doesn't play games.

God invites us to test him, to "taste and see that the Lord is good." God responds to sincere prayer. And God still does miracles. But God doesn't do tricks simply to tickle our fancy.

And don't even think about playing mind games with God. He not only hears what you ask, he knows why.

It's such a good thing he's on our side.

# One Way

"Do not let your hearts be troubled. Believe in God, believe also in me. In my Father's house there are many dwelling places. If it were not so, would I have told you that I go to prepare a place for you? And if I go and prepare a place for you, I will come again and will take you to myself, so that where I am, there you may be also. And you know the way to the place where I am going." Thomas [one of the original twelve disciples] said to him, "Lord, we do not know where you are going. How can we know the way?" Jesus said to him, "I am the way, the truth, and the life. No one comes to the Father except through me. If you know me, you know my Father also."

- The gospel written by John, chapter 14, verses 1 through 7 (John 14:1-7)

- New Revised Standard Version (NRSV)

- A disciple's account of Jesus preparing his closest disciples for his impending death. As was typical before they received the power of God's Holy Spirit (at Pentecost, Acts 2), the disciples were bewildered. The coming of his Holy Spirit gave them the understanding they needed.

# One Way

In many places in the Bible, Jesus refers to himself as the only way to God. This makes some folks unhappy. Seriously offended, in fact. So let's look at this.

First, Jesus never intended his words, "No man comes to the father except through me," to exclude anybody. These words are simply directions about where we can go to get the strength we need to live successfully. It's where we sense—know—God's presence in our lives and realize we have come home. This statement's about where to find our home.

Christianity moves us beyond a religious philosophy into a relationship with God. God's Spirit joins ours to become one. God shares our episodes of heavy lifting. God offers direction. And God sets the standards we need to live well. We are no longer alone.

We move from doing everything in our own strength to doing everything through God's strength. Our strength can fail, but with God's strength we can, as the Bible says, "do all things through Christ who strengthens me."

While there's only one way, nobody needs to be left out. The way is expansive enough to have room for everybody who chooses to walk it.

It's the way—and way of life—where we can walk with God.

# Ignorance Is Not Bliss

*H*ow sweet are your words to my taste; they are sweeter than honey. Your commandments give me understanding; no wonder I hate every false way of life. Your word is a lamp for my feet and light for my path.

- Psalm (rhymes with palms, p is silent) 119, verses 103–105 (Ps. 119:103–105)
- New Living Translation (NLT)
- Author uncertain, possibly King David. Psalm 119 is the longest chapter in the Bible. If you open your Bible at the middle, you'll land here.

# Ignorance Is Not Bliss

Scam artists depend on ignorance. And when it comes to the Bible, we accommodate them beyond their wildest dreams.

We know so little about the Bible that we believe whatever anybody tells us. And the line of anybodies ready to misinform us goes on for miles.

They tell us the Bible isn't a book of science. They fail to admit the Bible is accurate whenever it does speak scientifically. For instance, 3500 years ago Moses pointed the way to stopping the spread of communicable diseases. Amos wrote, 2700 years ago, of the seven stars of Pleiades—but only six are visible without a telescope, a much later invention.

They tell us the Bible isn't a book of history. And fail to concede the Bible's accuracy when it does speak of history. No archeological find has ever contradicted the Bible.

Worst of all, they tell us God has a mean streak and lurks somewhere the stratosphere—the great god of the gotcha. They fail to mention that God loves us no matter what. Or that God has big plans for us, plans for life's best. Or that our personalities, intelligence and talent are God's gifts to us to fit those plans. Or that God will never abandon us.

Don't depend on others to tell you what the Bible says. Find out for yourself. The news is far too good to leave to second-hand editorializing from shaky sources.

Ignorance is for patsies.

# BEYOND PHYSICS

*W*hen you were the slaves of sin, you were free from righteousness. What did you gain from doing the things that you are now ashamed of? The result of those things is death! But now you have been set free from sin and are slaves of God. Your gain is a life fully dedicated to him, for the result is eternal life. For sin pays its wage—death; but God's free gift is eternal life in union with Christ Jesus our Lord.

- Romans, chapter 6, verses 20 through 23 (Rom. 6:20-23)
- Good News Bible—Today's English Version (TEV)
- Paul's letter to the church at Rome. Paul was looking forward to his first visit to the church at Rome, but he arrived there in chains, imprisoned for his faith.

*S*ometimes there is a way that seems to be right, but in the end it is the way to death.

- Proverbs, chapter 16, verse 25 (Prov. 16:25)
- New Revised Standard Version (NRSV)
- "Wisdom sayings" of King Solomon, written about 931 B.C.

# Beyond Physics

God created the universe with both physical and moral laws. The physical laws we call physics. The moral laws we call morality.

People accept the physical laws. If somebody tries to defy gravity by walking off a tall building, we're not surprised by his fall. We don't blame an angry, uncaring God. "After all," we huff, "what did he expect?"

We teach our children the physical laws. We know a hand placed on a hot stove gets burned, so, to save them pain and possible scars, we warn our children about hot stoves. We accept, without a murmur, the fact that physical laws are not optional.

Moral laws are as immutable as physical laws. But, when we are detached from God, our human nature rejects even the concept of absolutes. We want no laws, no limits and no negative results.

Like children, we don't understand.

Knowing we don't understand, our loving Daddy, God, warns us about life's hot stoves throughout the Bible. He, too, wants to save us from painful burns and deep scars.

Rational people recognize the necessity of moral as well as physical laws.

Others persuade themselves that God's an old fuddy-duddy, the Bible's an outdated book and moral law is optional. They decide that right and wrong are individual decisions—but, when hurt, rage with bewilderment, angry that God allowed them to get burned.

Well, God warns us about hot stoves. It's up to us to listen.

# Don't Give Up and Don't Settle

*C*an anything separate us from the love Christ has for us? Can troubles or problems or sufferings or hunger or nakedness or danger or violent death? In all these things we have full victory through God who showed his love for us. Yes, I am sure that neither death, nor life, nor angels, nor ruling spirits, nothing now, nothing in the future, no powers, nothing above us, nothing below us, nor anything else in the whole world will ever be able to separate us from the love of God that is in Christ Jesus our Lord.

- Romans, chapter 8, verse 35 and verses 37 through 39 (Rom. 3:35, 37-39)

- New Century Version (NCV)

- Paul's letter to the church in Rome. Romans 8 shows Paul absolutely soaring in his greatest, most joyous expression of all Christ means to him. It's probably impossible to read this chapter and not get happy.

# Don't Give Up and Don't Settle

Marathon runners speak of "hitting the wall," when exhaustion sets in and their bodies scream for relief, begging them to stop. Knowing this will happen, most keep on keeping on.

Some runners finish poorly, most likely done in by a lack of training and conditioning. Some give in and quit.

Life's a lot like a marathon, and we all "hit the wall" from time to time.

From which point, some people half-heartedly stumble to the finish line. They take few, limited risks with extreme caution. They don't give themselves completely to anything ever again. They expected problems, but just one at a time. Fixable problems. Problems that didn't last too long. Some of them recover; some don't.

Others give up. They live in defeat and never risk again, whether to love, start a business or try anything new. They didn't expect life to be hard. They didn't condition themselves for maximum effort. At each fork in the road they took the easiest way, with a hope it would work out.

Victors get up and, fixing their eyes on the goal, strain to the finish line. Whatever happens, they don't give up. Even knowing the road will be rough and their muscles may knot in agony, victors continue the race with energy and determination. They struggle on to win the sweet taste of victory. They know when pain shrouds them like a black cloud, style points don't matter; it's finishing that counts.

We need to run after God with the same perseverance.

# It's All About the Finish Line

*M*eanwhile Saul [Paul] was uttering threats with every breath. He was eager to destroy the Lord's followers, so he went to the high priest. He requested letters addressed to the synagogues in Damascus, asking their cooperation in the arrest of any followers of the Way he found there. He wanted to bring them—both men and women—back to Jerusalem in chains. As he was nearing Damascus on this mission, a brilliant light from heaven suddenly beamed down upon him! He fell to the ground and heard a voice saying to him, "Saul! Saul! Why are you persecuting me?" "Who are you, sir?" Saul asked. And the voice replied, "I am Jesus, the one you are persecuting! Now get up and go into the city, and you will be told what you are to do." The men with Saul stood speechless with surprise, for they heard the sound of someone's voice, but they saw no one!

- Acts of the Apostles, known as Acts, chapter 9, verses 1 through 7 (Acts 9:1-7)

- New Living Translation (NLT)

- The story of Paul's conversion, a year or so after Jesus' death, from being an enemy of Jesus Christ to being a follower. Paul was familiar with Jesus and his teachings, but he refused to accept them until this dramatic encounter. In that era, Jewish men typically had two names—one for home and church (Saul) and one for everything else (Paul).

# It's All About the Finish Line

Paul is a giant personality in the Bible. He's a model of what Christians could be. He wrote most of the New Testament letters.

Which nobody could have predicted.

Paul appears on the scene shortly after Jesus' resurrection, at the beginning of the new church. Committing himself and his enormous intellect to being God's man, he rose quickly as a star in the church of his day.

Paul hated Jesus. He believes Jesus was a heretic and a phony, not the Messiah. He threw his life and money into destroying Christians. But God knew Paul truly wanted to serve God—and thought he was. Completely off course, he just needed a wake-up call.

One day, as Paul traveled to Damascus to find and imprison Christians, God knocked him down—literally. Temporarily blinded and lying in the road, he heard God's voice asking why he persecuted Jesus. As you might imagine, that experience changed everything.

Paul restudied the old prophesies and grew to realize Jesus was, in fact, the Messiah, the Christ. For the rest of his life Paul traveled widely, told everybody he saw about the good news of Jesus and started churches far and wide.

He was unstoppable. Beaten, thrown into prison, persecuted for his belief, he wrote that he counted it all joy because his relationship with God was worth any price. He had found the love, peace and satisfaction he yearned for.

As the saying goes, it's not where you start, it's where you finish. Paul finished well.

# CRASHING THROUGH LIFE

*T*hen he [Jesus] asked them [his twelve closest disciples], "Who do you think I am?" Simon Peter answered, "The Christ, the Messiah, the Son of the living God." "God has blessed you, Simon, son of Jonah," Jesus said, "for my father in heaven has personally revealed this to you—this is not from any human source. You are Peter, a stone; and upon this rock I will build my church; and all the powers of hell shall not prevail against it."

- The gospel written by Matthew, chapter 16, verses 15 through 18 (Matt. 16:15-18)
- The Living Bible (TLB)
- Matthew, one of Jesus' original twelve disciples, was present when Jesus told Simon Peter that these words he spoke would be the foundation for Christianity throughout history.

# CRASHING THROUGH LIFE

Peter was the leader in Jesus' inner circle of twelve. He spent the three years of Jesus' public ministry walking, talking, living with God in the person of Jesus.

A natural leader, larger than life, charging ahead without sufficient thought, daring great things, failing spectacularly, Peter gave life everything he had. Perfection, though, was not Peter's neighborhood. He always meant well, but his emotions frequently overruled his head, and he could go from the profound to the misdirected in a heartbeat.

On the profound side, Peter's declaration to Jesus, "You are the Christ, the son of the living God." is the foundation of the faith. But when the chips were down, he cursed Jesus and denied even knowing him.

Through it all Jesus took delight in Peter's heart for God. Above and beyond anything else, Peter wanted to be all God wanted him to be, and God can use somebody like that.

Jesus trusted Peter's heart more, even, than Peter did. The morning of his resurrection, just a few days after Peter cursed him, Jesus told Mary Magdalene to "go tell the disciples and Peter that you have seen the Lord." Jesus wanted Peter to know he was still on God's mind, still included in God's love. Peter went from there to greatness.

And believers through the years have taken comfort in Peter's lack of perfection. If God would love and empower Peter, we rightly reason, he must surely be willing to love and empower us.

*Truth is often more in the doing
than in the saying.*

# THE LIAR'S LIAR

*You* used to live just like the rest of the world, obeying Satan, the mighty prince of the power of the air. He is the spirit at work in the hearts of those who refuse to obey God.

- Ephesians (ee FEE zhunz), chapter 2, verse 2 (Eph. 2:2)
- New Living Translation (NLT)
- Paul's letter to the church at Ephesus (F uh suss)

# The Liar's Liar

Satan, the Bible says, is prince of this world. God rules the universe. We must choose which one we will serve, God or Satan.

We don't like this stark choice. From the outside, serving God looks boring, but serving Satan seems so, well, evil.

To make the choice seem benign—hopefully unnecessary—we trivialize Satan and make him red and cute, with horns and a tail. We tell jokes about him and insist he's easy to spot and tame.

More comfortably, we say he doesn't exist.

The truth is, Satan was once heaven's mightiest angel, expelled from Heaven for scheming to take God's place. The Bible says he's now a hungry lion stalking the earth in search of prey—which would be us.

Satan has great wisdom and sophistication. He's no match for God, but he's more than a match for us—attractive, charming, manipulative, a liar. In fact, Satan's the liar's liar. He plays with our minds. He makes his dead-end road look deliciously naughty and appealing, but choosing Satan means signing up for regret.

As he charms and beguiles us, Satan's unwavering intention is to destroy us. We laugh at that, thinking we're equipped to win his games, but we're outmatched in every direction.

God is the only power greater than Satan. God's Spirit in us is the only power that makes us winners over the evil determined to destroy us.

Truth makes the choice simple. Satan, of course, laughs at truth.

# Both a Giver and a Taker Be

*T*hen he [Jesus] said to the disciples [his followers], "Anyone who accepts your message is also accepting me. And anyone who rejects you is rejecting me. And anyone who rejects me is rejecting God who sent me."

- The gospel written by Luke, chapter 10, verse 16 (Luke 10:16)
- New Living Translation (NLT)
- The words of Jesus

*I*t is God's will that your good lives should silence those who foolishly condemn the Gospel without knowing what it can do for them, having never experienced its power.

- Peter's first letter, chapter 2, verse 15 (I Pet. 2:15)
- New Revised Standard Version (NRSV)
- A letter to the churches throughout Asia Minor from Peter.

# Both a Giver and a Taker Be

One way to group people is as givers or takers. While relationships require both, some people are heavy on the taking while others give and give and give.

Few people are all takers, fewer yet all givers. But there are those tendencies.

Takers size up any situation by "what's in it for me." The further into the taker camp they are, the more emphasis this gets. What's best for friends, relatives, country takes a distinctly secondary position. If, that is, they get a thought at all.

Givers are on the other end of the continuum. They focus only on what is best for others, even to their own detriment.

Gift-giving offers insight on the giver/taker balance. Takers choose gifts to make themselves look good, gifts to get off cheap, gifts they would like to receive, and so on. The needs and delights of the person receiving the gift get scant attention.

Givers focus entirely on the recipient, perhaps spending more than they can afford or taking time from essential duties to find the "perfect gift." Givers think only to please.

Absolute takers develop the soul of a prune and eventually destroy every relationship in their life. Absolute givers can be gullible dopes who wonder why everybody takes advantage of them. Neither absolute is where we want to be.

Jesus tells us to be "as shrewd as snakes, but as innocent as doves." God wants us in the giver camp—but he offers his wisdom so we're not dopes about it.

# BEING CLEAR ON WHAT IS ESSENTIAL

So now, since we have been made right in God's sight by faith in his promises, we can have real peace with him because of what Jesus Christ our Lord has done for us. For because of our faith, he has brought us into this place of highest privilege where we now stand, and we confidently and joyfully look forward to actually becoming all that God had in mind for us to be.

- Roman, chapter 5, verses one through two (Rom. 5:1-2)
- The Living Bible (TLB)
- Paul's expression of joy about his relationship with God through Jesus Christ.

# BEING CLEAR ON WHAT IS ESSENTIAL

John Wesley, one of Christianity's giants, said, "In essential things, unity. In unessential things, diversity. In all things, charity." (Love, to use current terminology.)

What are "essential things?"

The first essential is recognizing who Jesus is. Jesus is God breaking into history in human form, with human limitations, to complete man's understanding of God and pay the price for our sins. No other has been, is, or will be like him. God's word closes the door on any other interpretation.

False teachers attack the virgin birth, the basis of Jesus' perfection, although the Bible insists on it. They say Jesus never claimed to be God, although the Bible repeatedly reports that he did. They say we need a later, better revelation (their revelation) of God. They say Jesus didn't really die, although professional executioners on the scene verified it. They call the resurrection story a hoax, although Rome and the church hierarchy searched desperately to find Jesus' body and could not. Plus, a living Jesus appeared to hundreds after his resurrection.

It's all about ego. Their goal is to strip Jesus of his divine nature. If Jesus is only human, then they are his equal, and what they say is as valid as anything Jesus said.

They may tickle our ears for a time, but the deep hunger of our hearts remains. They have nothing real, nothing solid to offer. No love, no power, no wisdom and no guidance. Nothing.

Recognizing the real Jesus is essential.

# KNOWING WHO WE ARE AND WHAT TO DO

*And we know that in all things God works for the good of those who love him, who have been called according to his purpose.*

- Paul's instructional letter to the church in Rome, chapter 8, verse 28 (Rom.8:28)
- New International Version (NIV)
- Paul understands the concept of living by faith, that when we cannot understand how it could possibly be, we can depend on God to bring us to a solid place in life—even when negative things are happening. Notice, though, that the promise is conditional, limited to those who return God's love.

# Knowing Who We Are and What To Do

Another essential thing is recognizing who we are.

First, we need to realize we're sinners. We didn't become that way; we came that way. We can't fix ourselves, but God can.

Second, we're responsible for ourselves. Our life to date may have been difficult or it may have been easy. Whatever it was, it was. It's unchangeable, set in concrete. But our experiences brought us to where we are. As we walk with God, he "works everything together for good." He doesn't undo our past but uses it as he shepherds us to a good place.

Our responsibility is to wrap up our dreams, fears, hopes, pride, longings and disappointments—all the parts of our lives—and hand them to God. Then, as we follow his lead, we must allow God to work his changes in those dreams, fears, hopes, etc.

Third, we must positively persevere. Consider a baby learning to walk, enthusiastically exerting maximum effort and never giving up. Stumbling and falling aside, this is not work, but enthusiastically doing whatever it takes.

And we must understand we won't always understand. We don't need to know God's ultimate purposes. We only need to tackle the tasks and opportunities he puts in front of us.

Lastly, we need to believe God is for us. He' on our side. Our path won't always be easy and carefree, but it will lead our hearts to peace. And God will take each step with us.

# The Bible - Section #1

*I*n the beginning God created the heaven and the earth. And the earth was without form and void; and darkness was upon the face of the deep. And the Spirit of God moved upon the face of the water. And God said, Let there be light; and there was light.

- Genesis, chapter 1, verses 1 through 3
- King James Version (KJV)
- The Bible begins with the creation of the world. The phrase "moved upon" could also be translated as "brooded," as in a hen brooding her chicks. This tender expression gives us an idea of God's attitude of care toward his creation.

# The Bible - Section #1

The Bible contains two major sections, the Old Testament and the New Testament. The Old Testament is the first part of the Bible.

The Old Testament starts with the events of Creation. It tells the story of life from that time until a few hundred years before Jesus was born. Stories of courage, folly, love, loyalty, betrayal, suffering, wars, kings and kingdoms, relationships, successes and failures.

It is the history of man's growing understanding of God. How God revealed himself. The actions he took. The warnings he sent through his prophets.

It tells of the consequences of disobeying God. It speaks of his many promises—made and kept—to his children. It shows his power working through his people.

The Old Testament, written originally in Hebrew, isn't a continuous, year-by-year history, but a collection of thirty-nine books written by a wide variety of inspired authors, in many countries, over hundreds of years. There are books of history, poetry, guidance and prophesy. While most of the writers had no access to the thoughts of the others, all the books fit together without contradiction. Which, of course, is not humanly possible.

The Old Testament builds the foundation for the New Testament. Together they give us God's complete revelation of himself—who he is, what he does and what he expects of us.

# The Bible - Section #2

Now the birth of Jesus the Messiah took place in this way. When his mother Mary had been engaged to Joseph, but before they lived together, she was found to be with child from the Holy Spirit. Her husband Joseph, being a righteous man and unwilling to expose her to public disgrace, planned to dismiss her quietly. But just when he had resolved to do this, an angel of the Lord appeared to him in a dream and said, "Joseph, son of David, do not be afraid to take Mary as your wife, for the child conceived in her is from the Holy Spirit. She will bear a son, and you are to name him Jesus, for he will save his people from their sins." All this took place to fulfill what had been spoken by the Lord through the prophet: "Look, the virgin shall conceive and bear a son, and they shall name him Emmanuel, which means 'God is with us.'" When Joseph awoke from sleep, he did as the angel of the Lord commanded him; he took her as his wife, but had no marital relations with her until she had borne a son; and he named him Jesus.

- The gospel written by Matthew, chapter 1, verses 18 through 25 (Matt.1:18-25)
- New Revised Standard Version (NRSV)
- The good news of the beginning of Jesus' earthly life.

# The Bible - Section #2

The New Testament, the second part of the Bible, starts with the birth of Jesus. As in the Old Testament, the text comes in books. Here there are twenty-seven books originally written in Greek and Aramaic.

The first four books—Matthew, Mark, Luke and John—are called "gospels," which means "good news." The good news of Jesus Christ, God breaking into history in the final, completed revelation of himself.

Two gospels, Matthew and Luke, start with Jesus' birth and follow him through his life, death and resurrection. Mark and John start with Jesus' public ministry. John is written by theme; the others take a year-by-year approach.

The Acts of the Apostles, generally called Acts, comes next. It describes the early church. The apostles, including Jesus' disciples, led the early church.

Twenty-one letters come next. These letters, or epistles as they are called, were read publicly in the churches that were springing up everywhere. (In Acts, these churches are described as "the people who are turning the world upside down.")

The letters explain Jesus' teachings, describe how the Old and New Testaments fit together and teach about living a Christian life. They also address problems in the churches, which had people of every race, economic status and background trying to be united in their new faith—not much different from today.

The Bible ends with the book of Revelation, which symbolically describes Heaven, Hell and the end of this age, including Satan's final defeat in the lake of fire.

# Accurate But Impossible

---

*A*ll Scripture is inspired by God and is useful for teaching the truth, rebuking error, correcting faults, and giving instruction for right living, so that the person who serves God may be fully qualified and equipped to do every kind of good deed.

---

- The second letter to Timothy, chapter 3, verses 16 through 17 (II Tim. 3:16-17)
- Today's English Version (TEV)
- Paul's letter to Timothy, his "son in the faith," written just before Paul's death, traditionally believed to be by beheading. This was probably Paul's last letter.

# Accurate But Impossible

Although written by humans, the Bible is not a human document. It is the inspired word of God. Despite many different authors, in different places, in varying cultures, over centuries of time, it doesn't contradict itself.

When you consider its prophesies—all completely fulfilled, sometimes hundreds of years later—you know God was in charge. Indeed, over the ages, skeptics argued that some prophecies could not possibly be fulfilled. Until they were—accompanied by the sound of jaws dropping with astonishment.

We don't understand just how God worked in all of this. We only know the accuracy is beyond mathematical chance. Any possibility of random chance is overwhelmed by the Bible's consistency.

And, unlike the human approach to history and biography, the Bible shows reality, warts, wrinkles and all. For instance, David, ancient Israel's most revered king had amazing abilities—and amazing flaws. All are included. And Jesus said he would build his church on the faith of Peter, the leader of his disciples. But rather than a puff piece, the Biblical record details Peter's many mistakes, as well as his triumphs.

This combination of historical accuracy and clear-eyed view of the human condition gives us a completely dependable book. It's never been proven wrong. Accused, yes; proved, no.

And it is the record of extraordinary "coincidences" in the lives of ordinary people who walked with God. People like us.

*Our mountains are only dust bunnies to God.
Let him help.*

# Same Words, New Tune

*T*hree translations of The Gospel of John, chapter 1, verses 1 through 3 (Jn. 1:1-3)

In the beginning was the Word, and the Word was with God, and the Word was God. The same was in the beginning with God. All things were made by him; and without him was not any thing made that was made.
—King James Version (KJV)

Before anything else existed, there was Christ, with God. He has always been alive and is himself God. He created everything there is—nothing exists that he didn't make.
—The Living Bible (TLB)

When all things began, the Word already was. The Word dwelt with God, and what God was, the Word was. The Word, then, was with God at the beginning, and through him all things came to be; no single thing was created without him.
—New English Bible (NEB)

# SAME WORDS, NEW TUNE

The Old Testament was written in Hebrew. The New Testament was written in Greek and Aramaic. So, every English-language Bible is, obviously, a translation.

In translating from language to another, there are always words that give translators fits. Some words have no exact match in the new language, and the translator must decide which word fits best, if not exactly.

Translation is as much art as it is science. Different translators make different decisions. Translations by one committee differ from translations by another. The differences aren't huge, but they can throw you if you're not expecting them.

Also, as time goes on, words change their meaning, at times dramatically. A translation from years ago may seem to say something it never intended to.

Some translators move to paraphrases. In a paraphrase, whenever there is not an exact match for a word, the translator uses a phrase—even a paragraph—to make the meaning clearer.

The result is many, many versions of the Bible, each with its own fan club.

The Shakespearean language of the King James Version appeals to those of a Jacobean bent. Others prefer the simple language of the Good News Bible. The readability of The Message. And so on.

The various versions complement each other by saying the same thing in different ways. As you study the Bible, use several translations. The slightly different word choices make the original meaning clearer.

For everyday reading, the best version is the one you understand and look forward to reading.

# REAL CHRISTIANS GET DIRECTIONS

*B*less me with life so I can continue to obey you. Open my eyes to see wonderful things in your Word. I am but a pilgrim here on earth; how I need a map—and your commands are my chart and guide. I long for your instructions more than I can tell.

- Psalm (salm, rhymes with palm) 119, verses 17 through 20 (Ps. 119:17-20)
- The Living Bible (TLB)
- The author of this longest chapter in the Bible is uncertain. The Psalms are in the Old Testament, in the middle of the Bible. If you let a Bible fall open to the center, you will be in Psalms.

# Real Christians Get Directions

To grow as Christians, we must study the Bible. Children understand the basic stories easily, but understanding all the Bible offers takes at least a lifetime of study.

Here are notes to get started.

While the original text of the Bible was not divided into sections, books of the Bible are now divided into chapters and verses to provide an easy way to reference specific content. This book's Scripture excerpts illustrate the system.

Tables of contents tell you where to find each book.

"Study" Bibles have explanatory notes and descriptive headings for each section of text. A short discussion of the author, where and when the book was written, etc. starts each book. Time- lines show where the book fits into history and relate it to the other books of the Bible. You get maps, study guides, a topical index, and on, and on.

Some Bibles include a concordance which tells where specific words appear in the Bible. A concordance would show, for one example, each verse that includes the word "promise."

Bibles may have "chain references." These link verses on the same topic into a chain of references throughout the entire Bible.

Computer software helps, too. Software usually includes everything above plus several versions of the Bible for easy comparisons, commentaries on the text, famous sermons, historic writings, etc.

Joining a small study group helps, too.

Whatever tools you use, make the Bible a part of your everyday life. It has the directions you need.

# Finding a Home

*L*et us not neglect our church meetings, as some people do, but encourage and warn each other, especially now that the day of his coming back again is drawing near.

- The letter to the Hebrews, chapter 10, verse 25 (Heb. 10:25)
- The Living Bible (TLB)
- We are uncertain who wrote this intense letter that weaves together the Old and New Testaments, but it a graduate course in Christian living.

# Finding a Home

We live the Christian life as part of a community. Fellow-believers walk with us, learn with us, cheer our successes with us and mourn our losses with us.

We need this support group and family. Since we usually look for such a group while still in our spiritual infancy, some guidelines may help.

- *Openness*—A Christian group will not have secrets you can't share with outsiders or programs and ceremonies that nonmembers can't at least observe. You may not want to share every experience with non-church friends who may not understand them, but you must be free to do so.

- *Bible*—The Bible used for study and worship should be widely available in Bible bookstores. In study groups, a variety of Bible translations should be encouraged.

- *Authority*—No teaching, no book, no person—nothing—can be allowed to supercede the authority of the Bible. The Bible is God's word, affirmed by the life and words of Jesus, and it must be the ultimate authority.

- *Individuality*—God creates each of us to be unique. Authentic Christian groups accept, indeed welcome, individual differences.

- *Control*—Parents, teachers and clergy offer instruction and guidance, but our lives belong to God. He's in control.

- *Love*—The foundation for everything Christian is love. Not superficial, anything-goes, pseudo love, but genuine caring. People caring enough to welcome us and loving enough to help us grow and stay on track.

# HATE THE SIN, LOVE THE SINNER

There used to be false prophets among God's people, just as you will have some false teachers in your group. They will secretly teach things that are wrong—teachings that will cause people to be lost. They will even refuse to accept the Master, Jesus, who bought their freedom. So they will bring quick ruin on themselves. Many will follow their evil ways and say evil things about the way of truth.

- Peter's second letter, chapter 2, verses 1 through 2 (II Pet. 2:1-2)
- New Century Version (NCV)
- Peter's explains why knowing the Scriptures and understanding the power and presence of the Holy Spirit are so important to believers.

# Hate the Sin, Love the Sinner

The idea of loving a person while hating what they do confuses us.

We're supposed to follow God's example of loving people—and also his example in hating their sinful actions. Those actions separate them from God.

Separation from God is a dreadful thing, even for those oblivious of the price they're paying. We hate sin, then, because it costs too much and creates too much damage.

Then there's the part about loving sinners. This puzzles us, perhaps because of a misunderstanding of what love is. That word can mean so many things.

Greek, though, has different words for different types of love. *Philia* means brotherly love, which gives you a clue about where Philadelphia got its name. You might be interested to know that *Eros*, sexual love, doesn't appear in the Bible. *Agape* (ah GAH pay) is the Bible's ideal for love—the love that God gives us, unconditional love that insists on nothing in return. It is our goal.

Agape values people and encourages them to reach their best. It intends good for others. We agree with God that it is good—even wonderful—when love is returned, but the fact it may not be returned should not deter us from giving this gracious love to others.

Overlooking sin is sloppy agape, and wrong, but not loving sinners denies how precious they are to God.

So we hate the sin and love the sinner. It's not easy, but we get better with practice, and, fortunately, God shows us how it works.

# How To Get the Job Done

*A*nd now, just as you accepted Christ Jesus as your Lord, you must continue to live in obedience to him. Let your roots grow down into him and draw up nourishment from him, so you will grow in faith, strong and vigorous in the truth you were taught. Let your lives overflow with thanksgiving for all he has done.

- Colossians (kuh LAH shunz), chapter 2, verses 6 through 7 (Col.2:6-7)
- New Living Translation (NLT)
- Paul's letter to the church at Colossae (kuh LAH sigh), an inland city in the southwest of what is now Turkey.

# How To Get the Job Done

How does one become a child of God? A simple prayer does the job.

Time doesn't matter. God is open for business 24/7. Style doesn't matter. You don't need impressive words or a PowerPoint presentation. The only thing that matters is a sincere, repentant heart. If your heart is right, you're doing it right.

There's no fixed format, but if it makes you more comfortable to have a pattern, here is an example of a possible prayer.

> God, my life hasn't been all it could have been or should have been. I've done things I shouldn't have. I haven't done things I should have. So far, my life has made both of us less than happy.
>
> God, please forgive me for all my sins. (If it helps, list whatever bothers you.)
>
> Make me a new person. Make my soul clean. Give me a new start.
>
> Thank you for adopting me. I am now a child of God, God's Spirit and mine are one and I am a "new creation."
>
> Take charge of my life. Help me learn to hear your voice.

That's it! You're "born again," a spiritual baby in God's family. Heaven is celebrating. While, for the moment, you may or may not feel any different, your eternal life has begun. Now you start growing in God's wisdom and strength. Focus on God, nourish yourself with solid spiritual food and let it happen.

Have a great trip!

# Index of Articles

| Article title | Scripture | Page |
|---|---|---|
| A Brand New You | 1 John 3:1-2 | 17 |
| A Child of God | Psalm 8 | 4 |
| A Credible Witness | 1 Corinthians 15:9-10 | 91 |
| A Good Foundation Is a Solid Foundation | Proverbs 3:5-6 | 101 |
| A Modern Day Tale | John 3:1-6 | 55 |
| About This Forgiving Thing | Luke 17:3-4 ; 1 Peter 2:22-23 | 119 |
| Accurate But Impossible | 2 Timothy 3:16-17 | 159 |
| Always a Two-Way Street | 1 Corinthians 1:4-7 | 73 |
| Being Clear On What Is Essential | Romans 5:1-2 | 151 |
| Beyond Physics | Proverbs 16:25; Romans 6:20-23 | 137 |
| Big Ideas, Weak Knees | Psalm 139:1-18 | 67 |
| Both a Giver and a Taker Be | Luke 10:16 ; 1 Peter 2:15 | 149 |
| Castles In the Air | Isaiah 44:20 | 95 |
| Celebrating What Is | 1 Corinthians 3:1-2 | 25 |
| Comparative Confidence | Ephesians 2:8-10 | 99 |
| Crashing Through Life | Matthew 16:15-18 | 143 |
| Dead, Absolutely Dead | Matthew 27:62-66 | 87 |
| Designer Gods | Colossians 2:8-10 | 121 |
| Does Morality Count? | Ephesians 4:17-24 | 43 |
| Don't Believe Everything You Hear About God | Romans 1:19-21 | 103 |
| Don't Give Up and Don't Settle | Romans 8:35, 37-39 | 139 |
| Don't Travel Alone | Ephesians 3:14-19 | 105 |
| Everybody Believes In Something | Galatians 4:8 | 109 |
| Finding a Home | Hebrews 10:25 | 11 |
| First You Walk | John 1:12-13 | 23 |
| God Is Not Running For Sheriff | Galatians 6:7-8 | 107 |
| Grave Clothes | Matthew 27:57-60 | 85 |
| Growing Up Is Good To Do | Galatians 5:22-23; John 15:4-5 | 39 |
| Hate the Sin, Love the Sinner | 2 Peter 2:1-2 | 169 |
| Hearing God's Voice | John 16:13-14 | 31 |
| How Far Do You Want To Go? | Romans 8:1-6 | 53 |

| Title | Reference | Page |
|---|---|---|
| How To Get the Job Done | Colossians 2:6-7 | 171 |
| Ignorance Is Not Bliss | Psalm 119:103-105 | 135 |
| It's All About the Finish Line | Acts 9:1-7 | 141 |
| Jesus - An Introduction | Isaiah 53:5-6 | 69 |
| Knowing Who We Are and What To Do | Romans 8:28 | 153 |
| Learning To Hear | John 14:15-21 | 37 |
| Looking In the Wrong Direction | 1 Corinthians 1:20-21 | 79 |
| Maximum Defeat | Romans 5:8-11 | 83 |
| Moving On Up | Psalm 1 | 127 |
| Moving Past the Rule Pile | Exodus 20:1-17 | 27 |
| No Fence To Sit On | Luke 11:23 | 61 |
| Obviously, Rules Are Not Enough | Galatians 3:1-3 | 29 |
| On Being Unique | 1 Corinthians 12:12,14-22 | 77 |
| One Sunday Morning | John 20:18 | 89 |
| One Way | John 14:1-7 | 133 |
| Parlor Tricks | Luke 4:3-4 | 131 |
| Real Christians Get Directions | Psalm 119:17-20 | 165 |
| Same Words, New Tune | John 1:1-3 | 163 |
| Shifting Sands | Matthew 7:24-27 | 123 |
| Status and Power | Ephesians 1:16-19 | 117 |
| Strong Fingernails | Ephesians 3:20 | 57 |
| The Bible - Section #1 | Genesis 1:1-3 | 155 |
| The Bible Section #2 | Matthew 1:18-25 | 157 |
| The Big Choice | Luke 15:11-20 | 15 |
| The Daddy You Always Deserved | 1 John 4:15-18a | 3 |
| The Hold Of Habits | Romans 7:5-17, 24 | 51 |
| The Liar's Liar | Ephesians 2:2 | 147 |
| Throw Away the Scale | Colossians 1:19-22 | 111 |
| Trying To Put Jesus In a Box | 1 John 4:1-6 | 71 |
| Ungames | 1 Corinthians 1:18 | 35 |
| Walking Talks More Than Talking Walks | 1 Corinthians 4:20 | 45 |
| What Is This Thing Called Peace? | 2 Peter 1:3-4 | 9 |
| What Makes the Difference? | 1 Corinthians 1:13-16 | 19 |
| What's So Original About Sin? | Romans 3:22-24 | 7 |
| Where's the Power? | Matthew 6:9-13 | 47 |

| | | |
|---|---|---|
| Who Is Your Audience? | Galatians 1:10 | 115 |
| Who Leads and Who Follows? | Hebrews 11:1; Jude 14–15 | 59 |
| Who Qualifies? | John 3:16-17 | 13 |
| Who's In Control Here? | 1 Chronicles 29:11-13 | 75 |
| Why? | 1 John 4:9-10 | 63 |
| Why Bother | 1 John 5:1-5 | 93 |
| Working the Plan | 1 Corinthians 9:13-14 | 41 |
| You Can Count On Consequences | Matthew 5:23-24 | 125 |
| You Guilty Sinner You | 1 Samuel 1:7 | 11 |

# Index of Scripture References

| Scripture | Article title | Page |
|---|---|---|
| 1 Chronicles 29:11-13 | Who's In Control Here? | 74 |
| 1 Corinthians 1:4-7 | Always a Two-Way Street | 72 |
| 1 Corinthians 1:13-16 | What Makes the Difference? | 18 |
| 1 Corinthians 1:18 | Ungames | 34 |
| 1 Corinthians 1:20-21 | Looking In the Wrong Direction | 78 |
| 1 Corinthians 3:1-2 | Celebrating What Is | 24 |
| 1 Corinthians 4:20 | Walking Talks More Than Talking Walks | 44 |
| 1 Corinthians 9:13-14 | Working the Plan | 40 |
| 1 Corinthians 12:12,14-22 | On Being Unique | 76 |
| 1 Corinthians 15:9-10 | A Credible Witness | 90 |
| 1 John 3:1-2 | A Child Of God | 4 |
| 1 John 4:1-6 | Trying To Put Jesus In a Box | 70 |
| 1 John 4:9-10 | Why? | 92 |
| 1 John 4:15-18a | The Daddy You Always Deserved | 2 |
| 1 John 5:1-5 | Why Bother? | 62 |
| 1 Peter 2:15 | Both a Giver and a Taker Be | 148 |
| 1 Peter 2:22-23 | About This Forgiving Thing | 118 |
| 1 Samuel 1:7 | You Guilty Sinner You | 10 |
| 2 Peter 1:3-4 | What Is This Thing Called Peace? | 8 |
| 2 Peter 2:1-2 | Hate the Sin, Love the Sinner | 168 |
| 2 Timothy 3:16-17 | Accurate But Impossible | 158 |
| Acts 9:1-7 | It's All About the Finish Line | 140 |
| Colossians 2:8-10 | Designer Gods | 120 |
| Colossians 2:6-7 | How To Get the Job Done | 170 |
| Colossians 1:19-22 | Throw Away the Scale | 110 |
| Ephesians 1:16-19 | Status and Power | 116 |
| Ephesians 2:2 | The Liar's Liar | 146 |
| Ephesians 2:8-10 | Comparative Confidence | 98 |
| Ephesians 3:14-19 | Don't Travel Alone | 104 |
| Ephesians 3:20 | Strong Fingernails | 56 |
| Ephesians 4:17-24 | Does Morality Count | 42 |

| | | |
|---|---|---|
| Exodus 20:1-17 | Moving Past the Rule Pile | 26 |
| Galatians 1:10 | Who Is Your Audience? | 114 |
| Galatians 3:1-3 | Obviously, Rules Are Not Enough | 28 |
| Galatians 4:8 | Everybody Believes In Something | 108 |
| Galatians 5:22-23 | Growing Up Is Good To Do | 38 |
| Galatians 6:7-8 | God Is Not Running For Sheriff | 106 |
| Genesis 1:1-3 | The Bible - Section #1 | 154 |
| Hebrews 10:25 | Finding a Home | 166 |
| Hebrews 11:1 | Who Leads and Who Follows? | 58 |
| Isaiah 44:20 | Castles In the Air | 94 |
| Isaiah 53:5-6 | Jesus - An Introduction | 68 |
| John 1:1-3 | Same Words, New Tune | 162 |
| John 1:12-13 | First You Walk | 22 |
| John 3:1-6 | A Brand New You | 16 |
| John 3:16-17 | Who Qualifies? | 12 |
| John 14:1-7 | One Way | 132 |
| John 14:15-21 | Learning To Hear | 36 |
| John 15:4-5 | Growing Up Is Good To Do | 38 |
| John 16:13-14 | Hearing God's Voice | 30 |
| John 20:18 | One Sunday Morning | 88 |
| Jude 24-25 | Who Leads and Who Follows? | 58 |
| Lord's Prayer | Where's the Power? | 46 |
| Luke 4:3-4 | Parlor Tricks | 130 |
| Luke 10:16 | Both a Giver and a Taker Be | 148 |
| Luke 11:23 | No Fence To Sit On | 60 |
| Luke 15:11-20 | The Big Choice | 14 |
| Luke 17:3-4 | About This Forgiving Thing | 118 |
| Matthew 1:18-25 | The Bible - Section #2 | 156 |
| Matthew 5:23-24 | You Can Count On Consequences | 124 |
| Matthew 6:9-13 | Dead, Absolutely Dead | 86 |
| Matthew 7:24-27 | Shifting Sands | 122 |
| Matthew 16:15-18 | Crashing Through Life | 142 |
| Matthew 27:57-60 | Grave Clothes | 84 |
| Matthew 27:62-66 | Dead, Absolutely Dead | 86 |
| Proverbs 3:5-6 | A Modern Day Tale | 54 |

| | | |
|---|---|---|
| Proverbs 16:25 | Beyond Physics | 136 |
| Psalm 1 | Moving On Up | 126 |
| Psalm 8 | A Good Foundation Is a Solid Foundation | 100 |
| Psalm 119:17-20 | Real Christians Get Directions | 164 |
| Psalm 119:103-105 | Ignorance Is Not Bliss | 134 |
| Psalm 139:1-18 | Big Ideas, Weak Knees | 66 |
| Romans 1:19-21 | Don't Believe Everything You Hear About God | 102 |
| Romans 3:22-24 | What's So Original About Sin? | 6 |
| Romans 5:1-2 | Being Clear On What's Essential | 150 |
| Romans 5:8-11 | Maximum Defeat | 82 |
| Romans 6:20-23 | Beyond Physics | 136 |
| Romans 7:15-17, 24 | The Hold Of Habits | 50 |
| Romans 8:1-6 | How Far Do You Want To Go? | 52 |
| Romans 8:28 | Knowing Who We Are and What To Do | 152 |
| Romans 8:35, 37-39 | Don't Give Up and Don't Settle | 138 |
| Ten Commandments | Moving Past the Rule Pile | 26 |

*Don't share your dreams with just anybody. Be very, very selective, or they could get trampled in the mud.*

**Want more?**

**Get a free, e-mail quote-of-the-week every Monday morning!**

Go to www.ConfidentFaith.com

Sign up for "Quick Takes On Life"

An easy way to start each week with a 30-second thought to make you think—or laugh.

## Order additional copies of
## *How To Be A Christian Without Being Annoying*

**By mail:**    Confident Faith Institute
                PO Box 11744
                Glendale AZ 85318-1744
**By phone:**  800-235-4235
**By fax:**     623-572-5082
**On-line:**   orders@ConfidentFaith.com

| | |
|---|---|
| *How to Be A Christian Without Being Annoying* | $24.95 |
| Shipping & handling (U.S. and Canada) | 4.00 |
| Shipping & handling to other countries | 9.00 |
| Arizona shipments, please add sales tax | 2.02 |
| Total amount (U.S. funds, please) | |

| |
|---|
| Name: |
| Address: |
| |
| |
| E-mail: |

| |
|---|
| Check (Payable to Confident Faith Institute) |
| MC/Visa #: |
| Expiration date:         Code: |
| Signature |

*Quantity discounts available*